man alive!

Michael Green

Registrar, London College of Divinity
Northwood, Middlesex, England

INTER-VARSITY PRESS

130 north Wells, Chicago, Illinois 60606

INTER-VARSITY PRESS

Inter-Varsity Fellowship
39 Bedford Square, London WC1

Inter-Varsity Christian Fellowship
130 North Wells, Chicago, Illinois 60606

© INTER-VARSITY PRESS, LONDON

First Edition September 1967
Reprinted December 1967
Reprinted March 1968
Reprinted December 1968

UK *Standard Book Number: 85110 339 1*

Printed in Great Britain by
Billing & Sons Limited, Guildford and London

PREFACE

THIS BOOK is an examination of the basic claim of Christianity that Jesus Christ both rose from the tomb on the third day, and is alive today. It was prompted by this stricture by Lord Eccles, in his book *Half Way to Faith*, on the unintelligibility and irrelevance of so much theological writing: 'The laity, although better informed on almost everything else, have never been so ignorant about the ground-plan of the New Testament; this is partly your fault because you have concentrated your scholarships in fields too narrow to be widely interesting; will you now turn your attention to the gospel as a whole? to its relevance as a whole to the age in which we live?'

That seemed to me, as a theological lecturer, to be fair comment on a great deal of contemporary religious writing. Accordingly, I have tried in this small book, not indeed to produce anything so ambitious as an exposition of the relevance of the gospel as a whole to our generation, but at least an examination of its cardinal tenet, the resurrection. There are, of course, plenty of books on this subject, but most of them are content to treat the evidence for the resurrection without attempting to show its contemporary relevance, its challenge, its power to change men's lives, and the answers it gives to some of the most perplexing questions of our day. This is what I have attempted here. If it helps some people to a first-hand experience of the risen Christ, I shall be thankful, because the single most formative fact in my own life has been the discovery that Jesus Christ is not a dead historical figure, but a living person who can be met today.

Much of the material contained in this book is drawn from personal letters I have received from the individuals concerned. I have thought it best in most instances to avoid giving the names of my correspondents, but I am particularly grateful to them for providing the contemporary evidence without which this book could not have been written.

49964

CONTENTS

CHAPTER ONE

MORE DEAD THAN ALIVE

THE MODERN PREDICAMENT

IN 1945 WORLD WAR II came to an end. Everyone was determined that it must never be allowed to happen again. From now on we must build a better world, worthy of the tremendous sacrifices that had been made for Western civilization and its values, both by those who had died and those who had survived those gruelling years of combat.

But, somehow or other, that better world has not arrived. There are indeed many encouraging signs in contemporary society. There is a sense of justice which is violently opposed to racial discrimination; a sense of service which shows itself in voluntary work overseas; a sense of caring which is rightly indignant that the West should live in luxury while millions in the East hover on the brink of starvation. All these are signs of life in our society.

But in many other respects we are more dead than alive. We are better fed than ever, better paid, with better houses, better education, and splendid medical services. Conditions of work are easier, hours of work are shorter. One would have thought that the stage was set for a burst of vitality in the Western world which had rarely been equalled. Instead of that, we seem to be on the road to stagnation, to degeneracy. It is interesting that nobody writes books any more about ideal societies, Utopias. The flow, from Plato to Marx and H. G. Wells, has dried up. As people look into the future they write satirical, pessimistic pictures of what our monolithic, psychoanalysed, egalitarian society is likely to develop into. Aldous Huxley's *Brave New World* set the choice between freedom and happiness – and it ended with suicide. George Orwell's *1984* envisaged the end-product of a conformist society dominated by the Party's Thought Police, as utterly without hope, a world where there is neither freedom nor happiness, a world where men are more dead than alive.

Is that too pessimistic? Recently a national daily published a weekend supplement on what life might be like in England in 1990. For all the technological advance, it was an appalling picture. In a society where moral values no longer meant anything, the old folk were killed off, the family decayed, and boredom became the major national problem. Boredom is a killer. 'Nobody works more than 32 hours a week', continued the article. 'It is still common for middle-aged people to take to their beds, grow weaker and weaker, and after a few days, die.'

However exaggerated that account may be, there is truth in it. Although we have so much, we are not happy. Over half our hospital beds are taken up by patients suffering from psychological disturbance arising from the sheer strain of daily living, from guilt feelings, from inadequacy to cope with life, from loneliness. There is a general sense of disillusionment with politics, except at a General Election. The trade unions seem to elicit little more enthusiasm from their members. The number of men who really enjoy their work, and take a pride in it, is surely decreasing. Some do, of course; they may even live for their job. But for many it is merely the way of earning a living. The aim seems to be as much money as possible for as little work as possible. The job itself has gone dead on us.

But the really disappointing thing is that even money does not satisfy. It does not bring peace of mind or contentment. It usually makes us envious of others who have more. Keeping up with the Joneses is a very wearying business. Money cannot buy you love, respect, or indeed any of the things that make life most worth living. And a society which rates material prosperity as the highest good is finding increasingly that money and the things that money can procure do not bring lasting satisfaction.

It is obvious enough that there is a deadness, a breakdown of relationships, in society as a whole. There seems

6

to be a growing lack of understanding between many parents and their children. Increasingly, young people are fed up with home. It is impossible to calculate the appalling breakdown in marriage relationships, even if we leave on one side the 50,000 couples a year who end it in divorce. Only the other day I heard of a woman who had not spoken to her husband for ten years but left him notes when she had to pass him information! It is not without significance that most romantic pictures of marriage *end* on the wedding day: after that the picture is rarely so rosy. There's a deadness in many marriages.

Nevertheless it is widely believed that sex provides the most certain route to happiness. Surely here we shall find satisfaction? Never before has there been such widespread knowledge about the technique of love-making, coupled with so much sexual frustration. Intercourse outside marriage is now extremely common, and it does not satisfy. This was recently highlighted by the very popular film, *Alfie*. Alfie typifies the wide-boy, with no moral values, out only for his own gratification. And sex is the highway to this end. The story shows the breakdown in relationship between Alfie and each of his five women. It shows very graphically the futility of loose living. And it ends with Alfie standing on a bridge with a stray dog, asking in bewilderment, 'What's it all about?'

Hollywood is, perhaps, the clearest demonstration of the deadness of sex as an end in itself. In this, the richest six square miles in the world, where the average house costs £40,000, they have 1,912 swimming pools and an average family income of £7,000 a year. But they need 1,200 lawyers for the small population of 34,000 people; thirty-four private detective agencies; and no less than 172 psychiatrists! It was here that Marilyn Monroe lived and died. She was the sex symbol *par excellence* for millions of people. She had success, lovers, publicity, beauty and wealth. But in August 1962 she took an overdose of sleeping tablets to end it all. It was a Saturday night, and she was lonely. Marilyn Monroe warns us, if only we would listen, that sex will never bring lasting satisfaction, never make us fully alive.

7

Indeed, some of the avant-garde novelists recognize that this is a fact. Henry Miller is the foremost writer of this school, though there are plenty of film scriptwriters at his heels. In *Tropic of Cancer* and *Tropic of Capricorn* Miller has not merely written two sordid books; he has asserted that sex is dead, that the difference between men and women is meaningless. The growing cult of homosexuality appears to suggest that he is not alone in smashing sex.

There is a deadening in values, too. In the old days, people knew what was meant by right and wrong; today 'right' means 'what I want'. It is not 'wrong' to go to bed with someone else's wife, or to cosh a cashier over the head while robbing his till; it is only 'wrong' to get caught. Recent cases of car tax evasion, of the dodging of income tax, and of affluent people pilfering from shops emphasize the decline of honesty. It is hardly surprising in a society where virtue and religion are both pilloried in satirical programmes on the radio, where moral values are repeatedly declared to be relative and a personal matter, that crime should increase rapidly. That is just what we are experiencing. Crime among male adolescents has doubled in the past nine years; an even greater rise in crime figures is noticeable in girls between fourteen and twenty. There is an undeniable deadening of conscience amongst us

Perhaps the intellectuals are different? Perhaps this frustration, this deadness has not reached them? Indeed it has. Take a successful man of letters like Somerset Maugham. His dying words to his nephew Robin were, 'I've been a failure. I've had a wretched life. And I've made a hash of everything.' Malcolm Muggeridge, the author and broadcaster, described our 'morally appalling and spiritually impoverished affluent society' as 'no better than a pigsty'. He confessed, 'I do not believe that earthly life can bring any lasting satisfaction.' Ernest Hemingway committed suicide. Dylan Thomas died in despair. Men like this are no mere depressing exceptions to the general happy picture. Far from it. The problem of human dissatisfaction and restlessness is preoccupying many leading intellectuals. For Heidegger, the way in which a man authenticates his existence is by the deep dread and terror which he calls *Angst*. Jaspers, equally pessimistic, counsels his students against committing suicide in search of the 'final experience', in case, after all, it proves not to be final! To Sartre the universe is absurd, and this philosophy of life has influenced us all through Ingmar Bergman's films. Colin Wilson, author of the bestseller *The Outsider*, which is an acute enquiry into the sickness of mankind in the mid-twentieth century, summarized the tenets of many leading existentialist thinkers like this: 'Man is a useless passion. It is meaningless that we live, and it is meaningless that we die.'

Pop music reveals our unsatisfied quest for meaning, for relationship, for deep and lasting fulfilment, as a glance at any of the current top titles will show. The Beatles have produced particularly perceptive music. Their *Eleanor Rigby* song highlights the loneliness of modern man. 'All the lonely people. Where do they all come from?' It is a song about a young girl who lives and loves and dies in loneliness — and at her funeral Fr McKenzie preaches the sermon. 'No one hears. No one is saved.'

The current passion for drugs reveals the same lostness, the same despair. LSD, heroin, cocaine, as well as reefers and purple hearts, are enormously on the increase. Why? 'I was bored,' said one addict. 'Did it for kicks,' said another. 'What else is there to live for?' asked a third. The drug addict is the extreme example of twentieth-century man more dead than alive. He is only really 'alive' when he is 'high'. What a travesty of living!

These are some of the traces of death in our contemporary scene. It would be foolish to concentrate only on the brighter side of the picture, and gloss over the *ennui*, the boredom, the disenchantment which so many people feel. In an age of moral landslide, of political decline, of mass conditioning by press and TV, we are more dead than alive. For many people, joy in their work is dead, family relationships are dead, moral values are dead, and old-fashioned ideas like patriotism are simply laughable. It goes without saying that God is dead too. Instead of Bibles the bookshops stock horoscopes and almanacs. And, although we prefer not to think of it, physical death is the spectre that haunts the end of the corridor. We moderns do not know what to make of an idea like 'hell'; yet 'death' is only too meaningful. And all this a mere twenty-five years after the end of a great World War, which we hoped would end war and usher in a better world.

THE ANCIENT PREDICAMENT

It was a situation very similar to this which saw the rise of Christianity. In 31 BC the Battle of Actium brought to an end a century of civil war, which had wrought havoc throughout the known world. As in 1945, men were sick of war. They thought the Golden Age had come. Poets like Horace and Virgil wrote about it in glowing terms. They sang the praises of Augustus for bringing in the *Pax Romana*; they called him 'Saviour of the State'.

But a mere twenty-five years later, when Jesus Christ was born, men had grown somewhat disillusioned. Even on the political level, all was far from ideal. The price they paid for peace was increasing encroachment on the liberties of the individual, and a growing centralization in government, which left all too little room for local initiative. Political stagnation was the lot of most countries round the Mediterranean basin, for the simple reason that they were under the control, direct or indirect, of one man, Caesar Augustus. The only alternative was the Parthians and their barbaric ways – a horrible nightmare that constantly disturbed the slumbers of citizens of the Empire.

On deeper levels, the Golden Age was even more disappointing. It was a time of universal moral decline—orgies, homosexuality, obscenity of every kind. You have only to read Petronius' *The Banquet of Trimalchio* or Suetonius' *Lives of the Caesars* to get the flavour of dissolute Rome in the first century AD. The East had disgorged its filth into Rome, and immorality sapped the character of this once rugged and upright people.

On the religious scene, it was just as bad. The gods, if the poets were to be believed (and they were the theologians of the day), were as brutal, lustful, deceitful and greedy as mankind, utterly unworthy of men's worship. It is not surprising that many became virtual atheists, though they may have kept up occasional attendance at the great festivals of the gods. What did they put in the place of religion? Many turned to magic. Horoscopes were as plentiful then as they are now, and just as worthless. Papyri like this have survived: 'Saturn in triangular relation to Mars means bad luck. Venus in conjunction with Mars means fornication and adultery. If Mars appears in triangular relation to Jupiter and Saturn, this causes great happiness and enormous wealth.' Others who scorned magic and astrology turned to philosophy. But the philosophical schools were as barren in the first century with a diluted Stoicism and Platonism, as they are today with linguistic analysis. Seneca was one of the greatest philosophers of the time, and for all his emphasis on Stoic ethic, he began to admit its emptiness as he grew older. He came to share the despair of our contemporary existentialists. His admission that 'evil has its seat within us, in our inward parts' and that he was 'not even a tolerable man, let alone a good one' reminds me of Martin Buber's tragic cry, towards the end of his fine life of moral effort: 'Is there any force in the world that can change that intractable thing, human nature? There's a tragedy at the heart of things.'

The social scene in first-century Rome was equally disturbing. It was a time of great financial prosperity for the well-to-do. The upper-class Romans had enormous wealth through their estates and their overseas investments. Some of this wealth was gained by most questionable means: officials sent overseas to govern the provinces of the Empire enriched themselves shamelessly at the expense of the people they were supposed to serve. A most iniquitous tax system allowed various middle-men to take huge rake-offs, so that the poor citizen was almost taxed out of existence. The wealth of the 'haves' was balanced by the penury of the 'have-nots'. Moreover, slavery was eating the very heart out of the Empire. Some men owned as many as 30,000 slaves on their estates. And the slave had no rights, no redress at law. He was regarded simply as a piece of his master's property.

Above all, men were hag-ridden with fear. They feared being reported by a private snooper: an indiscreet word could mean ruin. They feared the Fates, through whom they thought their destiny was controlled. Supremely, men feared death. It was the great enemy waiting to snatch them up. Death was a subject that nobody cared to dwell on. There was little hope of life beyond. Catullus caught the mood of the majority when he wrote, 'Suns may set and rise again. When once our brief light has set, one unbroken night remains.' That is characteristic of the pagan attitude to death in the first century; it is characteristic of the non-Christian outlook today. A prominent British humanist put it succinctly, when he said, 'On humanist ideals life leads to nothing, and every pretence that it does not is a deceit.'

THE UNEXPECTED FACTOR

There is, then, considerable affinity between the situation which prevailed in the ancient world twenty-five years after the great deliverance of Actium, and the situation today, roughly the same period after an equally signal victory. A curious deadness haunted many sides of human activity. And then the unexpected happened.

Within two or three generations vast areas of the Roman Empire had discovered a new dimension to life. A new hope, a new zest for living, a new dynamism, a new and deep concern for other people began to show itself in every corner of the civilized world. It radiated out in concentric circles from an insignificant province on the edge of the Roman map, Palestine. This change was brought about not by any political edict, not by any social reform or cultural renaissance, but quite simply by the arrival in the world of Christianity.

Now Christianity as we know it in the organized

churches today could never have done such a thing. So fossilized, hide-bound and class-ridden a museum piece could never have swept such a breath of fresh air into the dying Roman civilization. The very idea is preposterous. The modern churches could, without gross exaggeration, be described as divided, cautious, conservative, introverted and dominated by their ministers. The early church was unquestionably united, bold, adaptable, outward looking, and every man was a missionary. Adolf von Harnack, in his great work *The Expansion of Christianity*, reminds us that 'the most numerous and successful missionaries were not the regular teachers, but Christians themselves, by their loyalty and courage. We cannot doubt that the great mission of Christianity was in fact accomplished by means of *informal missionaries*'. And Origen, writing at the beginning of the third century, commented, 'Christians do all in their power to spread the faith all over the world. Some of them, therefore, make it their business to wander not only from city to city but even to villages and hamlets to win fresh converts for the Lord.'

The early church's message was just as clear and dynamic as its members were. Today's church often burbles irrelevancies if it dares to burble anything at all. Its leaders speak with divergent voices. They talk, guardedly, about social matters. They talk, permissively, about morals. They write, learnedly, for learned theologians—nobody else takes the least notice. Christianity has often in the past appeared to be a code of behaviour: though even that is changing these days since immorality can now, we are told, under certain circumstances constitute a Christian virtue. Alternatively, it used to be viewed as a body of belief: though that too is on the way out since 'Christian atheism' came in. What, then, are the churches talking about these days? If one of the uninitiated ventured close enough to listen, he could be pardoned for supposing that the Roman Catholics were primarily concerned with priestly defections, Vatican II and birth control; the Anglo-Catholics would seem to be extremely anxious to ensure that the Methodist ministers got episcopally ordained; the Ecumenicals ardent for church mergers; the Radicals devoted to the New Theology and the New Morality; the Orthodox muttering about liturgy; the Pentecostals enthusing about speaking in tongues and the Conservative Evangelicals going on about sin. But where would he find the characteristic emphasis of the early church? It was, after all, their message that turned the world upside down. I doubt if anything less is likely to make much impression on our own contemporaries.

THE UNEXPECTED NEWS

What was the main emphasis of these early missionaries? It can be summarized in two words.

In a remarkable passage in Acts 17, we are told what the ordinary Athenian eavesdroppers understood Paul to be getting so excited about. Not politics, not bishops, not ecumenism, not even the cross. No, none of these things. He kept on talking about *'Jesus and Anastasis'*. The Authorized Version demurely renders this as 'Jesus, and the resurrection'; so do most of the other translations. That is to miss the whole point. The casual Athenian layabouts listening to Paul seem to have jumped to the conclusion that he was offering them an interesting couple of new gods for their pantheon, Jesus and his wife Anastasis. So great was his emphasis on Jesus and his resurrection.

I ask you, *could* anyone make a similar mistake today? I have yet to hear of a congregation complaining because its minister tells them too much about Jesus. And I have rarely met a minister who keeps on harking back to the subject of the resurrection.

But this is what Christianity is all about, according to these early preachers. It is essentially a relationship which people enjoy with Jesus Christ, who was once crucified, but subsequently rose to a new life. This was the discovery which so staggered Paul on the road to Damascus. Whatever doubts he had about Jesus during the carpenter-teacher's lifetime were settled decisively by the manner of his death—cruelly and crudely upon a Roman gallows.

14

Now the fact that Jesus was crucified told Paul two things. It made clear to him that Jesus could not possibly have been the Messiah, the great deliverer promised in so many strands of the Old Testament literature. For instead of leading Israel to victory over the Roman occupying forces, he had ended up in ignominious defeat. He was dead and gone. Consequently he could not possibly be the one they were expecting. And secondly, the crucifixion showed Paul, like anyone else who knew his Old Testament, that Jesus rested under the curse of God. Did it not say explicitly in Deuteronomy 21:23 that 'a hanged man is accursed by God'? On these two counts Paul considered Jesus to be a charlatan. Such a man nettled him. So he set out to hunt down his surviving followers. That is what he was doing on the road to Damascus when he had the shock of his life.

On that road he met with the risen Jesus. He was not expecting it: it was the last thing he wanted. But it happened. And it changed him from being a bitter antagonist to Christianity into being one of its most successful and devoted missionaries. That historic encounter taught Paul that he had made two mistakes. Jesus, he discovered, so far from being a Messianic failure, dead and gone, was alive and very much to be reckoned with. He appeared to him in the glory of God, and the sheer majesty of this blinded him.

Paul's other mistake was equally fundamental. He had thought that the death of Jesus on the cross meant that he rested under the curse of God. How could he possibly be wrong about this? Had he not got the authority of the Old Testament for his view? He tells us in Galatians 3:10, 13 that he was indeed not wrong in seeing that cross as the place of God's judgment. But he *was* wrong in thinking that because Jesus died there he must have paid the penalty for his own offences. He came to see that the death Jesus died was in some sense our death; he went to that place of judgment, of cursing, because of human wrongdoing.

This is very hard to understand, and I do not pretend to have got to the bottom of it. But the Bible is insistent that there is a link between wrongdoing and death. It comes as early as the account of Adam and Eve at the very beginning of the human story. They were told that if they disobeyed God and ate the fruit of the forbidden tree, they would die. They did eat. But did they die? I used to think that God was wrong and that the tempter was right after all when he promised them encouragingly in Genesis 3:4, 'You will not die', for they lived on pretty cheerfully for a long time. But I see now my mistake. *They did die, at once!* Up till that time, their lives had been lived in joyful companionship with God. From that moment onwards, he seemed to them to be a stranger. They were out of touch. They were expelled from the garden which they had shared with him. They were dead while they lived. And when they died physically, in the course of time, that merely put the lid on the living death they had been persuading themselves was life and liberty throughout a lifetime of disobedience.

Could this not prove to be the cause of our present human predicament? We *feel* dead as well as alive for the simple reason that we *are* dead as well as alive. Our wrongdoing, our wilful independence of God has cut the lines of spiritual life which bound us to him. We are spiritually dead whilst physically and mentally alive. The prime cause of the deadness we feel in so many sides of life is the deadness to our Maker which our disobedience has brought about. That is why St Paul writes to his Christian converts at Ephesus in these striking terms: 'And you he made alive, when you were dead through the trespasses and sins in which you once walked, following the course of . . . disobedience' (Ephesians 2:1, 2).

Christianity does not try to pretend that all is well with us; it recognizes the deadness which mars our life. It knows that such wilful disobedience richly merits the alienation from God, the loss of relationship and the separation involved in 'death'. But the amazing thing which Paul came to see is this. On the cross God himself stepped in, to put us in the right with himself again. Jesus, he gradually realized, was God as well as Man. And Jesus took upon himself the alienation, the lostness, the

16

spiritual death that properly belonged to us. Such was his love. He did indeed hang in the place of judgment, but the judgment he bore was ours by rights. As Man, he acted for the whole race. As God, his action has unending value. It avails for any man, anywhere.

And it was the resurrection which set God's seal on the whole business. The resurrection showed Paul that so far from resting under God's curse Jesus was in fact the key to all God's blessings. No wonder Paul went round the ancient world passing on this shattering discovery of a God who cared enough for us to stand in for us in the place of our greatest need. No wonder he insisted on preaching Jesus and the resurrection. In common with the rest of the Christians he had come into a new dimension to life. He could not keep quiet about it. He *had* to pass it on. For this Jesus, who died on a cross and rose again three days later, held the key to what life was meant to be, what it could be. Here was someone who was so fully alive that death could not hold him. This was news.

CHAPTER TWO

THE WITNESS-BOX

HOW ARE WE TO ACCOUNT for the beginnings of Christianity? What made it different from the Jewish religion from which it sprang? All the earliest Christians were, of course, Jews. What made them hive off from the religion of their fathers? It must have been something tremendous; we know today how tenaciously Jews stick to their faith, and it was the same in those days.

Clearly the moral teaching of Christianity is not enough to account for the birth of this new movement. Most of the teaching of Jesus, though arresting in form, was familiar to his Israelite hearers. His summary of the law, in Mark 12:29-31, to love God with all your heart and to love your neighbour as yourself, is the heart of Jewish orthodoxy itself. It is hardly an exaggeration to say that the earliest Christians had no new and distinctive system of morals, though perhaps they placed greater emphasis than other Jews on love. But it was certainly not the Sermon on the Mount that produced Christianity.

Nor was it the fact that they met separately, and became a sort of Jesus-synagogue. The Jews were very tolerant of different groups meeting separately within Judaism. It was not this that made Christians different. Indeed, we are told that for a considerable period they habitually went to the Temple and synagogues to worship with the other Jews who did not believe in Jesus.

No, there is only one thing that accounts for the start of Christianity, only one peculiarity they had which made them utterly different from others. It was this. They were convinced that Jesus was alive. Professor C. F. D. Moule of Cambridge puts it very clearly in *The Phenomenon of the New Testament*: 'From the very first, the conviction that Jesus had been raised from death has been that by which their very existence has stood or fallen.' They did not merely assert that the tomb of Jesus was empty on the first Easter day, though they did assert that. They also made it clear, both by what they said and what they did, that Jesus was alive in their midst. That has been the Christian faith ever since. Christians are convinced that Jesus is risen, and that he is willing and able to bring a new quality into the lives of those who are prepared to accept him.

FIRST-CENTURY WITNESSES

Even a cursory glance through the early chapters of the Acts of the Apostles shows the enthusiasm and vitality of this small band of a dozen dispirited Jews who, in disillusionment and despair, abandoned Jesus to his fate on the first Good Friday. 'They all forsook him, and fled,' we read in Mark 14:50. If they deserted him when he was still alive, it does not take much imagination to see how

18

unlikely it is that they should seek to further his cause when he was already dead. But by the opening chapters of the Acts a remarkable change has come over these disciples. They are new men. They have something of vital importance to say, and they do not care what risks they run in telling it.

On the first day of Pentecost, just seven weeks after the execution of their leader, they caused a tremendous disturbance in the very courts of the Temple. People thought they were drunk. Peter replied to this effect, 'That can't be true. It is too early in the day to be drunk! But what God promised long ago has come true. He has given us his Spirit, the Spirit that lived in the prophet Jesus— whom you wickedly killed, but whom God wonderfully raised from the tomb. *This* is what accounts for the change you have noticed in us.' Such was the thrust of Peter's speech: he and his friends were, as he puts it in Acts 2:32, witnesses of the resurrection. And three thousand Jews were convinced by what he said and became Christians on that day (Acts 2:41).

In Acts 3 we find Peter and John healing a paralysed man. Everyone was astonished. But the apostles emphatically disclaimed any credit for the cure; it was due to Jesus. They said, 'You . . . killed the Author of life, whom God raised from the dead. To this we are witnesses' (Acts 3:15). They did, however, maintain that Jesus offered men not only new power for old limbs, but new pardon for old sins. 'God, having raised up his servant, sent him to you first, to bless you in turning every one of you from your wickedness' (Acts 3:26).

This did not please the religious authorities; enthusiasm rarely does. They immediately imprisoned the apostles. Such teaching was highly impolitic in the contemporary balance of power: just the sort of thing to annoy the Romans. In any case, it could not be true. The Sadducee ecclesiastics did not believe in any resurrection; they were too enlightened. So they proposed to put a stop to this nonsense forthwith. The apostles were herded into prison. But the number of believers crept up to five thousand (Acts 4:3, 4).

What next? Well, the authorities tried to overawe the offending apostles by an impressive council meeting. But all the joy they got out of that was this bold rejoinder from the prisoners in the dock: 'By the name of Jesus Christ of Nazareth, whom you crucified, whom God raised from the dead, by him this man is standing before you well . . . And there is salvation in no one else, for there is no other name under heaven given among men by which we must be saved' (4 : 10 ff.). The discomfited members of the San-hedrin saw the radiant courage of the Christians. They recognized the mute witness of the healed man, standing quietly there to attest the reality of Jesus' risen power. And they could say nothing against it. So they tried to browbeat the apostles into silence—but it was a vain hope. 'And with great power the apostles gave their testimony to the resurrection of the Lord Jesus' (Acts 4 : 33). It is not surprising that they were held in great esteem by the crowd. They had come alive.

Gone were the crippling inhibitions which had kept them quiet in the previous seven weeks; they now preached ceaselessly. Gone was the cowardice which had kept them hidden away in an upper room; they were now as bold as brass for what they knew to be true. Neither prison, perse-cution, nor the threat of death could silence them. In point of fact many of them did seal their testimony with their blood. The consciousness of the risen Christ in their midst made a difference even to their basic instinct for private ownership, and they shared their possessions with one another in a practical and loving communism. There is no doubt about the witness of these earliest Christians in the very heart of Judaism, Jerusalem itself. It made a profound impression. Their lives as well as their lips asserted that Jesus was indeed alive.

What was true in Jerusalem was equally true in the pagan areas which Christianity transformed with its gos-pel. Corinth is a notable example, for we know a good deal about the church there through Paul's two long letters to them. Corinth was a boom town, which had flourished and expanded during the eighty years since it was refounded. It was an important trading city, and a major seaport. Its name was a byword, even in the lax culture of the day, for flagrant immorality. Cult prostitution took place in the temple of the goddess of love, and many of the men who later became Christians had once indulged in orgies of this sort. But now they were new men, reclaimed by the power of Christ's Spirit which had come to take up residence inside them. Paul writes in 1 Corinthians 6:9 ff.: 'Neither the immoral, nor idolaters, nor adulterers, nor homosexuals, nor thieves . . . will inherit the kingdom of God. *And such were some of you.* But you were washed, you were sanctified, you were justified in the name of the Lord Jesus Christ and in the Spirit of our God.'

Now that is a very remarkable thing. Such men had been abandoned, shameless pleasure-seekers, interested only in fulfilling their own lusts. But it was out of *these men* that Jesus created his church in Corinth! Washed in a baptism made effective by Christ's atoning death on the cross, their past was dealt with. And the Spirit of the risen Lord now lived in their bodies, as though they were his temples. That is both the reason and the dynamic for their spectacular change of behaviour. If the gospel of the risen Lord could do that for the rakes of Corinth, then it spoke volumes for the truth of the resurrection.

In this same letter Paul includes the earliest piece of evidence on the subject to be found anywhere in the New Testament. The letter itself was written a mere twenty years after the events of that first Easter, which in itself is impressive enough, but the material he quotes takes us much further back than that. This is what he writes: 'First and foremost, I handed on to you the facts which had been imparted to me: that Christ died for our sins, in accordance with the scriptures; that he was buried; that he was raised to life on the third day, according to the scriptures; and that he appeared to Cephas (*i.e.*, Peter), and afterwards to the Twelve. Then he appeared to over five hundred of our brothers at once, most of whom are still alive, though some have died. Then he appeared to James, and afterwards to all the apostles. In the end he appeared even to me . . .' (1 Corinthians 15:3–8, NEB).

21

Paul is quoting. The repeated 'that' tells us as much. He is quoting from something very old, a tradition which calls Peter by his Aramaic name of Cephas. It must, therefore, have arisen in the earliest Christian community while it was still Jewish. But most interesting of all, Paul is quoting a formula which was *already traditional before he became a Christian*. The words he used, 'handed on' and 'imparted', are, both in Greek and Hebrew, the terms used for the official transmission and reception of tradition. We have here, that is to say, embedded in Paul's first letter to Corinth, a summary of the Christian belief about the resurrection which was traditional by the time of Paul's conversion. And that could not have been more than three or four years after the death of Christ. Accordingly this tradition must emanate from the first year or two of the Christian era. It is, therefore, of incalculable value as evidence of the earliest Christian witness.

This ancient piece of teaching does not attempt to prove the resurrection. It tells us the simple facts of Jesus' death, burial and resurrection. It points out that this was in accordance with the Old Testament Scriptures (a fascinating point which we shall examine later), and then proceeds to give us eyewitness testimony from a stream of witnesses. That, of course, is the way you substantiate any supposedly historical happening. You cannot prove it; but you can amass so much eyewitness testimony that only the prejudiced would refuse to credit it.

What, then, are these witnesses claiming? They are not saying that they have seen Jesus rise from the dead. Nobody in the New Testament claims that. This is, incidentally, one of the marks of their truthfulness. Anyone making up the story could hardly have resisted claiming to have been present at the actual resurrection. In point of fact, some of the second-century apocryphal Gospels make just this claim. But not the earliest Christian witnesses. They make a more sober but at the same time more far-reaching claim.

They bear witness to the fact that Jesus not only rose, but is *alive*. This comes out clearly from a glance at the tenses used in this passage. 'Died', 'was buried' and 'ap-

peared' are all in the aorist tense, the normal tense for a
past action. But the verb translated 'he was raised to life'
stands out like a sore thumb, for it is in the perfect tense.
And the perfect is used when a past event has effects that
remain until the present. So in that single word *egegertai*
we see two crucial points. Not only did he rise on the third
day, as a fact of history; *he is still alive*, and that is something that can continually be verified. Such was the
earliest Christian assertion about the resurrection: a
matter of history and a matter of experience.

Now this is a staggering claim. What witnesses does this
ancient fragment of tradition adduce to support it?

First, 'he appeared to Cephas'. We do not know what
passed between them on this occasion. Perhaps it was too
personal for publication; Peter had let his Master down
so badly that his restoration was an intensely private
affair. The event is referred to, with the same tantalizing
reserve, in Luke 24: 34. But leaving aside the contents of
that interview, I should want to know, if I were cross-
examining this witness, what accounts for the astounding
change in him. How is it that the cowardly fellow who, at
the trial of Jesus, shrank from the gossip of a maidservant,
turned into the courageous leader who took a major part
in founding the early church, in the face of tremendous
opposition, and, in the end, endured crucifixion for his
Master? I should want to know what changed him from
that boastful, hot-blooded disciple we read of in the Gospels, to the modest, gentle, mature Christian leader who
confronts us in every page of his first Epistle, and had such
quiet confidence in God that he could sleep peacefully
amid an armed guard when he knew he was to be executed
the next morning (Acts 12: 6)? I fancy he would find one
single word sufficient answer to my questions: *Egegertai*,
'He is alive'.

Secondly, the Twelve come before us to give their
testimony. How is it that they, the pathetic little group
who all forsook Jesus and fled at the time of his greatest
need, are such changed men? How have they turned,
almost overnight, into the indomitable band of enthusi-
asts who braved opposition, cynicism, ridicule, hardship,

23

prison and death in three continents, as they preached everywhere Jesus and the resurrection? Their answer would be simple: *Egegertai*, 'He is alive'.

A surprising witness is then brought forward, James. Now James was a member of Jesus' family, one of the sons of Joseph and Mary (Mark 6: 3). Did he always believe in the claims of his brother? Was he a follower of Jesus during his public ministry? Emphatically not. As a matter of fact, in common with his other brothers, James not only disbelieved in Jesus, but he thought he was somewhat deranged (John 7: 5; Mark 3: 21). It is almost inconceivable that a man who took this attitude to one of his own family whilst he was alive should have changed sides dramatically after Jesus' execution. Yet that is precisely what happened. James became a believer. He became a leader in the Jerusalem church. What did it? There can be no doubt about that. 'He appeared to James.' It was the resurrection that changed the Lord's brother from cynic into Christian.

Before we leave this interesting list of witnesses we must hear what those five hundred Christians have to say. Some of them had died in the twenty years since the events of the crucifixion and the resurrection, but most of them were still alive to give their testimony at the time when Paul wrote, about AD 53. We know nothing more about them. They are the forerunners of the hordes of nameless Christians who have been bearing their witness to the same truth ever since. So let us examine them. 'Are you concerned to say that on a certain day you saw Jesus alive after his death? Is *that* it?' we might ask. 'No,' they would reply, 'that is not the main point. On such and such a day we did indeed meet Jesus, alive again from the tomb. But to us the greatest thing is that he is with us still, though we cannot see him. He shares our very lives. He talks with us and we with him every day. He has come by his Holy Spirit to take up residence in our personalities. He is no past hero to us. He is our living contemporary and companion. Our great aim is to allow him to control and transform our characters, and to use us in introducing others to God.'

From that day to this, Christians have maintained this truth. Jesus did not only rise from the tomb; but he is alive, our contemporary.

I well recall the day when as a teenager I first made this discovery. I had believed in the fact of the resurrection, in a second-hand way, all my life; but it meant nothing to me in practice, until a few months earlier, when I came across some boys and masters at school to whom the living Christ clearly meant a great deal. They had a joy, a poise, a vitality, a good humour and an unselfishness which greatly impressed me. I wanted it too. And then that Sunday afternoon a friend showed me that if Jesus rose, then it followed that he was alive. So I could meet him, and come to know him. Hesitantly, then, I put my life in his hands, as best I knew how. And I have proved the reality of his presence ever since. It has gradually become the greatest certainty of my life.

'Oh,' you say, 'it's all very well for you. But you're a parson!' True enough. But I would never have dreamed of becoming one had I not found that Jesus is alive. However, I shall be glad to call some twentieth-century witnesses who are not parsons.

Michelle is a white South African graduate, a highly intelligent mathematician. She was born into a Jewish family, but in the course of her studies at Cape Town University had been impressed with the Christians she knew. She came on a houseparty where I was the visiting speaker, and during those days she encountered the risen Christ for herself. Later, she wrote to tell me of her baptism. She described the service, which she managed to persuade her father to attend, and then she continued: 'I think this is one of the most wonderful facets of Christianity, the great joy it brings. When I was telling someone else about it over the phone, they said they could *hear* how happy I sounded . . . Before my baptism I was scared to admit to my Jewish friends that I was a Christian, but now I want the whole world to know.' This joy is not some froth which speedily wears off; the excitement of the early days of relationship with the risen Christ gives way to a deep and lasting contentment, a contentment which is maintained as the Christian is willing to obey his Master's leading wherever it may take him in the service of others. Michelle has found this in the two years of her Christian discipleship, and she is now actively engaged in Christian work at home. Others find their love for Christ takes them to other countries.

Recently I was having supper with a brilliant doctor friend. He won most of the important medical prizes at university and hospital. He got his F.R.C.S. at the first attempt. The way to Harley Street stood invitingly open, particularly as he already had family connections there. But Graham was a follower of Jesus Christ. He was accustomed to sharing his decisions great and small with his risen Lord. And he felt the call of Christ to Nepal. So he went. And he is now deeply happy to be sharing the good news of a risen Saviour with the Nepalese, who, as a nation, were entire strangers to the Christian gospel until a few years ago. There is nothing starry-eyed about this sort of discipleship. It is harshly realistic, and it is very costly. But those who take the risen Christ at his word find that his promise holds firm, 'I am with you always' (Matthew 28 : 20).

You do not have to have been born in a Christian environment to begin the adventure of Christian living. There is a fascinating growth of Christianity in Russia where for over a generation very great atheistic pressure has been brought to bear. I am told that almost all the younger priests in the Orthodox church in Russia were once atheists. Their encounter with the risen Lord has stood the test of determined anti-Christian indoctrination whilst they served in the armed forces. This, in itself, is a remarkable present-day testimony to the truth of the Easter faith.

A professor from behind the Iron Curtain told me this simple but impressive story. It concerned a Polish girl who lives in Warsaw. She comes from a militantly atheistic home. Somehow or other she got invited to a meeting of Christian teenagers in Warsaw, and was fascinated by their evident joy as they spoke of Jesus. Soon afterwards she happened to sit next to a Christian on a bus. He spoke to her quietly of his risen Lord, and, secretly, she believed. She found in her own heart the reality of which the others had spoken, and after a week, she plucked up courage to tell her parents. They were, predictably, furious. She was kicked out of house and home. But it made no difference to her peace of mind, her quiet but evident joy, and the manifest change in her life. The result? Her parents are now enquirers. They want what she has got.

The dynamic change that made new men of the first disciples is equally evident today, where the risen Christ is fully trusted. An American drug addict, delivered from the grip of heroin addiction by the power of Christ, expressed himself like this. 'No, not drugs, liquor, or anything else can give me the peace of mind I have in Jesus. I wouldn't trade this Christian life for anything in the world. Thank you, Jesus.' This may sound somewhat extravagant, but it is obviously completely genuine. I have myself had a great deal to do with a heroin addict who has progressively been liberated from the passion for the drug by Jesus Christ, and it has been a joy to see the gradual reclamation and undreamed-of development of a character who was well set on the road for an early death from heroin poisoning. It was a reminder to me of the intense relevance of this message of the risen Jesus to one of today's most intractable problems.

Many young people who are impatient with organized religion are deeply aware of how unsatisfied they are; and they are quick to notice when a friend of theirs somehow becomes different. I was struck recently, after preaching at a student service, by the following shrewd comment from a young man who joined a queue of enquirers. When I got to him, I asked him why he had stayed. He said something like this: 'I've had nothing to do with the church, but I'm intrigued by the life that a Christian student leads. He shares digs with me. So I thought I'd come along, and see what makes him tick.' What did make his friend tick is exactly the same thing that this medical student is trying to express: 'I knew a lot about Christianity before I finally became a Christian. The last thing that decided me was seeing the life of two Christian friends. They were always cheerful, and seemed to have a peace of mind I did not have. I could almost *see* Christ living in them.'

This is the sort of witness that many of our contemporaries bear to Jesus Christ, though they are a small minority, as Christians have always been. They speak of what they actually know from their own experience of Christ. That may not seem very satisfactory; it would be much tidier if the thing could be proved one way or the other. But such is life. It is not possible to put satisfactorily into words an experience which has changed your life, let alone prove it. That is what a Ghanaian undergraduate found. 'I know Jesus lives, because I meet him every day, and share fellowship with him. Fellowship can exist only between people who are *living*. I think that the truth that Jesus lives is something that one can experience rather than describe.'

That is very true. And it is borne out by this story a Czechoslovakian theologian told me. A Russian lecturer, a member of the Communist party, was addressing a packed audience on the subject of the resurrection of Jesus Christ. He spoke at considerable length, seeking to discredit it. At the end, an Orthodox priest rose and asked if he might reply. He was warned that he could only have five minutes. 'Five seconds is all I shall need,' was his reply. He turned to the audience, and gave the delightful Easter greeting, characteristic of the Eastern Orthodox. '*Christos anestē*,' he cried, 'Christ is risen.' Back with a deafening roar came the traditional reply from the crowded hall, '*Alēthōs anestē*', 'Truly he is risen.'

That is the essence of the Christian witness down the centuries. From the first century until today, among rich and poor, educated and simple, black and white, it is the same. Christians all bear witness to this truth that Jesus is risen and alive. Surely this is a claim that merits very serious attention as we turn in the next two chapters to consider the historical question, Did he really rise?

CHAPTER THREE

THE FACTS OF THE CASE

SO FAR IN THIS BOOK we have concentrated on *experience*. This has been quite deliberate. Lots of people who have no interest in arguments, theology or historical research are very interested in Christianity if it can be shown to be relevant to daily living. That is why I have approached this central question of the Christian faith, the resurrection, from the standpoint of experience. But this must not obscure the fact that the really basic question is not 'Does it work?' but 'Did it happen?' And this question of evidence is what I propose to examine in the next two chapters. The resurrection is either true or false. It should be possible, by careful examination, to reach a conclusion. Did Jesus rise from the tomb, or did he not?

There is no lack of evidence. On the contrary, the very variety and complexity of it is baffling. If only we had a professional investigator, a Sherlock Holmes, to guide us! It is just the sort of case he would be delighted to take up —criminal, mysterious, and exceedingly important. How would he go about it?

KEEP AN OPEN MIND

Holmes would never go into a case with his mind made up before he had scrutinized the evidence. He would tell us to beware of bringing to the case dubious assumptions which militate against an impartial enquiry. These tend to be of two sorts, theological and scientific.

Theological prejudice

The theologians tend to assume that they can have the Easter faith without the Easter event. Jesus' body may still be mouldering in a Palestinian tomb, they think; but we can nevertheless share his quality of life. To regard

Jesus not as a dead memory but as a living presence neatly sidesteps the historical question of whether he left that tomb on Easter day or not. And that is very convenient. It rescues Christian faith from historical enquiry! Some professors tell us that we should not need empty tombs and resurrection appearances to bolster up our faith in the risen Lord. Indeed, they insist, it is quite wrong to bolster up *faith* with *history* in any shape or form. In any case, we are told, it is impossible to get behind the Gospels to what actually happened: for the Gospels were all written by men who shared the Easter faith, so their testimony cannot be trusted. Furthermore, the resurrection cannot strictly be called a historical event (and thus be subject to the normal rules of evidence), because history as we know it is bounded by death. If Jesus rose, this must have been by an act of God, and acts of God are not accessible to historical investigation, only to the eye of faith.

Now there is a lot of sense in all this. It is a healthy reminder that the most important thing about the resurrection is not an empty tomb in Palestine two thousand years ago, but the risen Lord today, whom we can meet and know for ourselves. It is a healthy reminder, too, that you cannot *prove* that anyone is alive by historical enquiry, only by meeting them. All this is splendid. But it can never banish the proper question, 'What actually happened?' Christianity is unashamedly a historical religion. It claims God came to share our life, to die for our sins, and on the third day to rise again. If he did not, then the Christian faith is false. It is as simple as that. The empty tomb can assuredly not 'prove' the reality of the risen Lord today. But equally, Christian experience cannot be encounter with the 'risen' Jesus if he is still mouldering in that grave. Whilst, therefore, we must rid ourselves of the idea to be found in some older Christian apologists that the empty tomb, if established, could prove the resurrection of Christ; we must equally firmly resist the convenient but dishonest dead end, advocated by some modern apologists, of maintaining airily that the empty tomb is irrelevant to Christian faith. The Bishop of Woolwich, in his book *But That I Can't Believe,* asserts, 'But the empty tomb is not the resurrection any more than the shell of the cocoon is the butterfly.' Quite true. But without the cocoon there is no butterfly! It is illicit to claim that Jesus is a living presence and at the same time be sceptical about the empty tomb. If you are agnostic about the historical resurrection, you are necessarily very vague about the Spirit of Jesus which is supposed to dwell in you. As the learned German Professor Pannenberg rightly says, 'The outlook for Christianity would be bleak if the resurrection of Jesus was in reality not an historic fact.' History cannot demand of us the personal commitment of faith, but it does give the grounds for such commitment. We cannot sit loose to history. We cannot, therefore, rest content with any theological short cuts. We must examine the evidence.

Scientific prejudice

The second presupposition, which makes dispassionate examination of the resurrection difficult for most of us, is scientific. It is simply this. Dead men do not rise. There is no class of events known to us in which such a thing can be catalogued. The resurrection story, therefore, *cannot* be true.

This attitude is not common among leading scientists, many of whom are themselves Christians. But it is common among ordinary people who have been influenced to a greater or lesser degree by the scientific method, which has had such remarkably successful results in our own generation. Now the scientific method is unashamedly inductive. That is to say, it does not begin with theories about what ought to happen. It begins by examining what does, as a rule, happen, and then goes on to frame its generalizations (or 'natural laws', as we rather grandiosely call them). These may be, and indeed *have been*, revised in the light of further evidence. The whole thing is eminently practical and empirical. You begin with the facts, and see where they lead you.

That is precisely what I am asking you to do. That **is**

what Holmes always did. Examine the evidence and see where it leads you. That is the scientific method. From the very nature of the case there are no parallels to the resurrection. We are not talking about the resuscitation of a corpse: this has been done for a limited period with a number of men, and subsequently they always die. We are talking about the resurrection to an immortal life of one who claimed to be God incarnate. You would not expect such a unique figure necessarily to conform to the pattern we have come to acknowledge as normal for other men. Jesus is in a class by himself. It is certainly within the realms of possibility that such a man could not be held captive by death. We must examine the evidence.

EXAMINE THE EVIDENCE

Jesus was dead

The first thing Holmes would do, having cleared Dr Watson's mind of prejudice, would be to go to the scene of the crime. That is, unfortunately, denied us, but we have such plentiful evidence from those who were on the scene of the crime shortly after the reputed resurrection, that it is not difficult to ascertain the main facts.

It is not a pleasant story. An innocent man has been judicially murdered, with the connivance of the religious and secular authorities, and the backing of public opinion. After a sleepless night, in which he was given no food, endured the mockery of two trials, and had his back lacerated with the cruel Roman cat-o'-nine-tails, he was led out to execution by crucifixion. This was an excruciatingly painful death, in which every nerve in the body cried aloud in anguish.

He died in an unusually quick time, six hours or so. The four executioners came to examine him, before a friend, Joseph of Arimathea, was allowed to take away the body for burial. These soldiers were experienced at their grisly task: crucifixions were not uncommon in Palestine. They knew a dead man when they saw one—and their commanding officer had heard the condemned man's death cry himself and certified the death to the governor,

Pontius Pilate (Mark 15: 39, 44). But just to make doubly sure, they pierced his heart through with a spear. And then a very remarkable thing happened.

We are told on eyewitness authority that 'blood and water' came out of the pierced side of Jesus (John 19: 34, 35). The eyewitness clearly attached great importance to this. Had Jesus been alive when the spear pierced his side, strong spouts of blood would have emerged with every heart beat. Instead, the observer noticed semi-solid dark red clot seeping out, distinct and separate from the accompanying watery serum. This is evidence of massive clotting of the blood in the main arteries, and is exceptionally strong medical proof of death. It is all the more impressive because the evangelist could not possibly have realized its significance to a pathologist. The 'blood and water' from the spear-thrust is proof positive that Jesus was already dead.

Jesus was buried

After his death was certified, Jesus was taken down from the cross and buried in a rock tomb nearby, belonging to a secret disciple, Joseph of Arimathea. The body was placed on a stone ledge, wound tightly in strips of cloth, and covered with spices. St John's Gospel tells us that some seventy-five pounds were used, and that is likely enough. Joseph was a rich man, and no doubt wanted to make up for his cowardliness during the lifetime of Jesus by giving him a splendid funeral. The amount, though great, has plenty of parallels. Rabbi Gamaliel, a contemporary of Jesus, was buried with eighty pounds of spices when he died. But details like this make nonsense of the theory that Jesus was not really dead, and that, revived in the cool of the tomb, he crept out and persuaded his gullible disciples that he was risen from the dead.

This rationalistic refuge from the strong evidence for the resurrection has a long ancestry. It was produced by Schleiermacher in 1799 and was revived recently by Hugh Schonfield in *The Passover Plot*. But it would not detain

33

a competent detective long. It ignores the deadly character of Jesus' wounds, the careful examination by experienced Roman executioners, the blood and water, the constricting graveclothes, the crushing weight of spices, the lack of human help, and the sealed tomb. What is more, it is psychologically impossible. How could someone who crept half-dead out of a tomb, needing bandaging, strengthening, and every care, someone who subsequently died in obscurity, have given the impression that he was Lord of life and conqueror over the grave?

The tomb was empty

He was dead and buried. We can be sure of that. Now the united testimony of the earliest Christians is that on the third day the tomb was empty. Matthew, Mark, Luke, John, Peter, the Virgin Mary and Mary Magdalene are unanimous on the matter. So, by inference, is Paul.

Now it is often said that Paul knows nothing of the empty tomb, and that as his writings antedate the Gospels, this calls the matter seriously in question. It is certainly true that St Paul is much more interested in the risen Jesus than he is in the emptiness of his tomb. But there are three pieces of evidence in our earliest document, 1 Corinthians 15, which show that Paul was very well aware of the fact that Jesus' grave was empty.

In the first place, he quotes as of prime importance the very early piece of tradition which we examined in the last chapter, that he was raised to life *on the third day*. What does this tradition imply? It must mean here, as in Acts (*e.g.*, 10:40), that on the third day the tomb of Jesus was found to be empty, and Jesus was met, alive. The mention of that third day is decisive. It shows Paul knew about the empty tomb.

Secondly, when *Jews* spoke about resurrection, they meant only one thing. They did not mean the survival of the soul, for the Hebrews regarded human personality as a unity. They meant *bodily resurrection* when they spoke of resurrection. They would not know what to make of the spiritual survival which is what some modern writers want to attribute to St Paul's understanding of Christ's resurrection. To a Jew, if Jesus' bones were still in a Palestinian tomb, there could be no argument about it. He was not, in that case, risen. Throughout 1 Corinthians 15 Paul asserts the reality of the resurrection in the most robust terms. He was a Jew, and could not exclude the physical from his understanding of 'resurrection'. You can search the Rabbinic writings in vain to find any mention of a purely spiritual resurrection. Furthermore, when you recall that all the earliest believers in the risen Christ were Jews, when you remember that 'a great many of the priests were obedient to the faith' (Acts 6: 7), then it is simply naïve to claim that a 'spiritual' understanding of the resurrection will cover the facts. When Paul said 'risen', he meant 'physically risen'. 'If Christ has not been raised, your faith is futile and you are still in your sins. . . . If in this life we who are in Christ have only hope, we are of all men most to be pitied' (1 Corinthians 15: 17 ff.).

The third piece of evidence that Paul took the empty tomb for granted, and simply assumed it without argument, is this. He goes to some lengths to explain, in the second part of that long chapter, that our destiny is to be made like Christ. We shall have a resurrection *body*, as Jesus had. 'Just as we have borne the image of the man of dust, we shall also bear the image of the man of heaven . . . this perishable nature must put on the imperishable, and this mortal nature must put on immortality' (1 Corinthians 15: 49, 53). Just as the physical body of Jesus was transformed at the resurrection, so it will be with the Christian. This sort of analogy would be utterly impossible if Jesus' body was not raised.

There can be no doubt, then, that Paul knew the tradition of the empty tomb and accepted it without bothering to discuss it. On the third day the tomb was unoccupied, because God had raised Jesus to a new life, beyond the reach of death.

At this point it may be relevant to examine two bits of pagan evidence which bear, rather surprisingly, on this case. Josephus, a Jewish historian, writing at the end of the first century AD, has this fascinating passage in *An-*

tiquities, 18.3.3. 'Now there was about this time Jesus, a wise man, if it be lawful to call him a man; for he was a doer of wonderful works, a teacher of such men as receive the truth with pleasure. He drew over to him many Jews, and also many of the Greeks. This man was the Christ. And when Pilate had condemned him to the cross, upon his impeachment by the principal men among us, those who had loved him from the first did not forsake him, *for he appeared to them alive on the third day*, the divine prophets having spoken these and thousands of other wonderful things about him. And even now, the race of Christians, so named from him, has not died out.' Attempts made to show that Josephus could not have written this have failed. The manuscript tradition is uniform. And we know that this passage was in the text of Josephus used by Eusebius in the fourth century. It is possible that one or two slight textual emendations should be made, but the substantial authenticity of what Josephus wrote is unassailable, and has been reiterated by the most recent Loeb edition of his works. And it is all the more remarkable when we remember that, so far from being sympathetic to Christians, Josephus was a Jew writing to please the Romans. This story would not have pleased them in the slightest. He would hardly have included it if it were not true.

The other piece of pagan evidence is even earlier than Josephus. It is called the Nazareth Inscription, after the town where it was found. It is an imperial edict, belonging either to the reign of Tiberius (AD 14–37) or of Claudius (AD 41–54). And it is an invective, backed with heavy sanctions, against meddling around with tombs and graves! It looks very much as if the news of the empty tomb had got back to Rome in a garbled form (Pilate would have had to report: and he would obviously have said that the tomb had been rifled). This edict, it seems, is the imperial reaction.

There can be no doubt that the tomb of Jesus was in fact empty on the first Easter day. The only other alternative will not stand investigation for a minute. It was proposed by Kirsopp Lake that, in their overwrought state, the women visited the wrong tomb in the dim light of that Easter dawn, and were directed to the right one by the words of a young man who happened to be around early, and realized their mistake: 'You seek Jesus of Nazareth, who was crucified . . . he is not here; see the place where they laid him' (Mark 16:6). The women were, of course, terrified and ran away. Later they made the young man out to be an angel, and his words to be an announcement of the resurrection.

Ingenious, but it will not do. For one thing, it leaves out the crucial words the young man is reported to have said, '*He has risen*, he is not here.' For another, it is not very convincing to suppose that the three women who had so lovingly and courageously attended to the last rites of Jesus on the Friday evening should, a mere thirty-six hours later, all have been mistaken about the location of the grave they themselves had helped to prepare. Indeed Mark almost seems to go out of his way to anticipate this objection by ending his account of the Friday evening thus: 'Mary Magdalene and Mary the mother of Joses took a good long look at (such is the meaning of *etheōroun*) where he was laid' (Mark 15:47). But the complete refutation of the theory is very simple. If the right tomb was known, why on earth was the right body not produced, as soon as the resurrection began to be preached? That would have scotched the new movement at the start. But that is what nobody could do. The body was not to be found.

WEIGH UP THE ALTERNATIVES

Having established that Jesus was really dead and buried, and that his tomb was empty on the third day, the implications of these facts must now be faced. Why was the tomb empty?

One possible explanation

If someone moved the body of Jesus, the field of suspects is fairly restricted. Only the enemies and the friends of

37

Jesus would have had much interest in the case. Let us suppose, then, that the chief priests removed the body to a place of safer custody, to prevent Jesus' tomb becoming a place of pilgrimage.

But would they? He had claimed that he would rise from the dead, and they remembered that claim. This is clear from one of the accusations at his trial: 'We heard him say, "I will destroy this temple that is made with hands, and in three days I will build another, not made with hands"' (Mark 14:58). This is clearly a garbled account of something Jesus actually said. Perhaps the true account is preserved in John 2:18-21, in which Jesus was referring to his body by the words 'this temple', and the whole statement looked forward to the resurrection. We are told that some of his disciples remembered this subsequently. It seems that some of his opponents did, too.

And then there was the request the Jewish leaders made to Pilate for a guard on the tomb. 'Sir,' they said, 'we remember how that impostor said, while he was still alive, "After three days I will rise again". Therefore order the sepulchre to be made secure until the third day, lest his disciples go and steal him away, and tell the people, "He has risen from the dead", and the last fraud will be worse than the first' (Matthew 27:63, 64). Would the chief priests, who went to all this trouble to prevent anyone from tampering with the body, have been so incredibly foolish as to lend colour to the idea of the resurrection by removing it? They had, at long last, got Jesus where they wanted him, dead and buried. They were interested only in keeping him there. Of course, if by any chance they had been so misguided as to remove the body, they could easily have rectified the situation by triumphantly producing it when the Christians started spreading the story of the resurrection. Instead, they could only order them to be silent. We may be very sure that the enemies of Jesus did not take his corpse from that tomb. That possibility can be ruled out.

If his enemies did not rifle the grave, what about his friends? Why should they not have removed the body? Surely this is the most plausible explanation?

Plausible it may be; but there are two good reasons why it is false. They *could not* have done it if they wanted to, and they *would not* if they had been able to.

The disciples could not have removed the body of Jesus for the very simple reason that there was a guard on the tomb. It is fashionable to disregard the account of the guard, on the grounds that it is only recorded in St Matthew's Gospel, and in any case looks like Christian propaganda. To my mind, however, it rings true. It is attested, quite independently, by two of the apocryphal Gospels of the second century and by intelligent Christian writers like the philosopher Justin and the lawyer Tertullian, also in the second century. Furthermore, it is just what you might expect to happen, given the mixture of law and intrigue that went to make up the administration of the province of Palestine. The body of a condemned criminal remained Roman property. That is why Joseph had to go and ask no less a person than the Governor for it, if he wanted to give it burial. And as soon as Pilate had said 'Yes', the whole situation changed. The body was now back in Jewish custody. Responsibility for any riots that ensued would fall fairly and squarely upon Jewish shoulders. That is what made the chief priests pluck up courage to brave the Governor once again, when they knew that he was in a black mood, in order to try to persuade him to place a guard. They were playing the age-old game of passing the buck. But Pilate refused to be drawn. He said to them, 'You *have* a guard of soldiers; go, make it as secure as you can' (Matthew 27:65). They had, indeed, the Temple Police. Their plan to evade responsibility had failed; ruefully they set their own guard, having failed to get his! But this did not prevent the tomb being empty on the third day.

So afterwards the priests had to produce the lame story of the watchmen sleeping on duty while the Christians made off with the corpse. Not very good for morale, but better than admitting the resurrection!

How anyone could suppose this story arose in Christian circles for apologetic reasons has always astonished me. The resurrection needed no such bolstering to these early disciples. They were far too sure of the reality of the risen Lord in their midst to go round inventing stories of how his tomb came to be empty. In any case there are two tell-tale words in the account which settle the matter – *hēmōn koimōmenōn*, 'while we slept' (Matthew 28:13). No Christian could have made *that* up and put it in the mouth of the guards. The story would only have been of any use for Christian propaganda *if the guards had stayed awake*!

The only conceivable reason why the story got around, therefore, was that it was true. There had been a guard. It had not proved effective. And it was bribed by the Jewish authorities to say that the disciples came and stole the body while they slept. The guard makes it very difficult to suppose that the friends of Jesus could possibly have removed the corpse.

In any case, would they have done so? The suggestion is absurd. It is clear from all the accounts that the disciples were utterly disheartened men. They were anxious only to run away, hide, and forget all about the whole affair. They had been on a wild goose chase in following Jesus of Nazareth, and the crucifixion had dashed all their hopes. They had no thought of carrying on his cause. Resurrection never entered their heads.

But even if it were possible to credit these eleven men with such cunning at the moment of their greatest disappointment, what are we to make of the sequel? They were soon joyfully proclaiming the resurrection all over the world, and nothing could stop them. Prison, torture and death could not alter their conviction that Jesus was alive. No, the theory that the disciples stole the body is psychologically untenable. It does not explain the facts. They could not have stolen it if they would – because of the guard on the tomb. They would not if they could – because of their subsequent behaviour. It was Maurice

Goguel who disposed of this theory more tersely than anyone else I know. *'On peut se laisser persecuter pour une
illusion,'* he wrote, *'mais non pour une fraude'* – Men
might indeed be willing to die for a passionately held
illusion: but not for a piece of flagrant deception.

An important clue

Sherlock Holmes would be driven to exclude these sug-
gested explanations for the empty tomb, even though he
might not yet be able to suggest any acceptable alternative. But I can imagine him going away to brood over the
significance of a point of detail, which would not have
escaped his eagle eye.

It concerns the graveclothes. We are told that the graveclothes were left behind in the tomb. One wonders why, if
the body was pilfered by either friend or foe. But there is
more to it than this. There is an eyewitness account, contained in St John's Gospel, which says of Peter and John:
'Simon Peter came, following him, and he went into the
tomb; he saw the linen cloths lying, and the napkin,
which had been on his head, not lying with the linen
cloths but rolled up in a place by itself . . . and he [John]
saw and believed' (John 20: 6–8). Why should this have
made such an impression on John? For this reason. The
wrappings were like a chrysalis case when the butterfly has
emerged: undisturbed, but empty. Those tightly wound
bandages had encased Jesus as closely as the chrysalis case
fits round the pupa inside. The turban round his head
would, of course, have been separate from the wrappings
round his body: that, too, was empty. But, like the graveclothes, it still retained the shape it had when twirled
around the head of Jesus. This is what made such a profound impression on John. It almost seemed as though
the body of Jesus had vaporized, and had passed through
the graveclothes. Those which had covered his body were
intact (apart from the fact that they were crushed by the
weight of spices, now that there was no body inside),
whilst the turban kept its original concave shape. What
could account for such a strange phenomenon? No grave-

41

robber would have been able to enact so remarkable a thing. He would simply have taken the body, grave-clothes and all. Had Jesus merely been resuscitated, he would presumably either have used the clothes or laid them aside. But as it was, the signs all pointed to Jesus having been raised to a new order of life, a new sphere of existence. And he had left the graveclothes behind, as the butterfly emerging to a new dimension of life leaves behind its cocoon. That sight convinced Peter and John. It provides food for thought to any careful investigator.

On-the-spot examination of the scene of the crime would have given Holmes a lot to think over. The indications, improbable as they might seem, pointed to the possibility that Jesus might after all have been raised from that tomb by God. It would be important to keep a close watch on further developments.

CHAPTER FOUR

MAN ALIVE!

IF THE MYSTERY of the missing body of Jesus had ended with the discovery of an empty tomb, an investigator would be justified in looking for some natural explanation, however far-fetched. But it did not end there. In fact, that was only the beginning. Within a few days of his execution, all sorts of people were claiming that they had seen Jesus alive again. We met some of them in chapter two: the Twelve, who knew him so well; James, his incredulous brother; Thomas, the sceptic; Paul, the violent opponent; and the five hundred Christians who saw the risen Christ on the same occasion. These appearances continued for some six weeks, and then stopped. Ten days after the last appearance, on the day of Pentecost, just fifty days after this strange business all began at Pass-over-time with the crucifixion, Jerusalem was again in uproar over Jesus. His followers began preaching with quite phenomenal confidence that he was alive. Nothing could quench their zeal. They were prepared to face any hazard in proclaiming that God had raised Jesus from the grave, that he was the conqueror of death, and that he was worthy of man's worship and allegiance, since the resurrection had proved that his claims to deity were well founded. *That* was the surprising sequel to the empty tomb.

STRANGE APPEARANCES

Investigation would have informed a Holmes that these appearances began on the third day after Jesus' execution on the Friday: that is to say, they began on the Sunday, for the Jews reckoned numbers inclusively. This in itself would have caught his interest. Why the *third* day? Indeed the whole business of the numbers is odd. Would anyone making up the story have invented such awkward delays—resurrection on the *third* day, appearances for *forty* days, and public proclamation only after *ten* further days had elapsed?

How did these appearances all begin? Jesus was reputed to have revealed himself first of all to one of the grief-stricken women who had come to embalm his body, Mary of Magdala. She took him for the gardener, it appears, and then, convinced by the way in which he pronounced her name that it really was Jesus, she fell at his feet in worship. Jesus would not let her touch him, but sent her back to the disciples with the news. Such was the story. Not very impressive, one might think: an emotional woman, dazed with bereavement, might easily imagine such a thing when confronted with the empty tomb. And yet, the very vulnerability of the story says something for its truth. After all, if you were going to spin a cock-and-bull story about the resurrection of your hero, would *you* lay yourself open to ridicule by making the first witness to his new lease of life a hysterical woman?

Later that day two disciples were trudging sadly along the road to Emmaus, a village near Jerusalem. They were discussing the devastating event of the crucifixion, the end of all their hopes. Let Luke continue the story in his own words. 'As they talked and discussed it with one another, Jesus himself came up and walked along with them; but something held their eyes from seeing who it was. He asked them, "What is it you are debating as you walk?" They halted, their faces full of gloom, and one, called Cleopas, answered, "Are you the only person staying in Jerusalem not to know what has happened there in the last few days?" "What do you mean?" he said. "All this about Jesus of Nazareth," they replied, "a prophet powerful in speech and action before God and the whole people; how our chief priests and rulers handed him over to be sentenced to death, and crucified him. But we had been hoping that he was the man to liberate Israel"' (Luke 24 : 15 ff., NEB).

That was the characteristic attitude of all the disciples: sad, thoroughly discouraged. They were not expecting to see their master again. They reckoned his cause was lost. Holmes would conclude that the resurrection could not possibly be wish fulfilment.

One of the very interesting features of these appearances is that Jesus was never recognized instantaneously. There was always something just a little different about him. These two on the way to Emmaus did not take in who it was until Jesus' characteristic knack of breaking bread at table revealed his identity to them without the possibility of mistake. Needless to say, they raced back to Jerusalem with the news, only to find the disciples agog with the report that Peter, too, had met Jesus. While they discussed the matter, Jesus himself stood before them. Again that note of awe and amazement is struck. They were terrified out of their wits, and they thought they were seeing a ghost. To convince them that he was no ghost, Jesus invited them to handle him; and he ate some broiled fish and honeycomb before their wondering eyes (Luke 24 : 42 f.).

Thomas was not with them on this occasion, and he stoutly refused to believe a word of it. We should be grateful to him for his determination not to be taken in, because his doubts occasioned another appearance of Jesus a week later. Jesus invited Thomas to put his finger in the marks left by the nails, and to thrust his hand into the spear-wound in his side so as to assure himself that it really was he. We are not told whether Thomas tried the experiment. At all events he was completely and utterly convinced, and gave voice to the deepest expression of faith to be found in the New Testament, 'My Lord and my God!' To which Jesus responded with those memorable words, 'Have you believed because you have seen me? Blessed are those who have not seen and yet believe' (John 20: 28, 29).

These men were no simpletons. We tend to think, 'Poor things, they did not have our standards of critical judgment.' But that is to forget that they no more expected to see a dead man walking around than we would. They were, in fact, just as incredulous and hesitant as we would have been. The same initial doubt features in almost all the accounts of the appearances – and they number twenty and more. But once they were convinced, they never doubted again. Instead, they turned the Roman world upside down with their preaching of Jesus and the resurrection.

Were these fabrications?

What are we to make of these appearances? Were they made up by the early Christians? Once again we come up against this stubborn fact that men do not suffer and die for a lie. And if they had made these stories up, they would hardly have left so many ragged ends. It is exceedingly difficult to make a coherent sequence of the appearances recorded in the four Gospels and 1 Corinthians 15. While this remains a nuisance for the tidy-minded harmonizers, the artless lack of collusion does back up the reliability of the events themselves. The early Christians were convinced that they had seen Jesus risen. Some had done so in Jerusalem, some in Galilee, where he had promised to meet them before his death; others on the Damascus road, and the Emmaus road; by the seashore, in the garden,

The very variety and lack of homogeneity in these stories militate against their being fabrications. Had they been making it all up, the Gospel writers would have made sure that the stories tallied exactly. They would have produced eyewitnesses of the resurrection itself, of the Lord breaking the bands of death. They would have made sure that the appearances were either all of a spiritual Jesus or of a resuscitated, tangible Jesus – not a curious mixture of the two. It would all have been very different. We may be confident that these stories were not made up.

Or hallucinations?

But could not the early Christians have been subject to some sort of hallucination? This, again, is possible in theory. Those who suffer from hallucinations find them every bit as 'objective' as other experiences shared by normal folk.

There are, however, serious obstacles to accepting this account of the matter. Normally you find that a particular type of person is subject to hallucinations. Someone like Mary Magdalene might fill the bill, but hardly people with the diversity of temperament and disposition of James, Paul, Thomas and Peter! Normally, moreover, hallucinations are very individualistic things. A man may believe that he is Napoleon, but it is rare to find that many people from very different backgrounds all suffer from the same delusion. Here the same phenomena are reported by fishermen, tax-gatherers, close relations, and five hundred people at once.

Again, it is normal to find people getting hallucinations about things they have been hankering after for ages. The wish becomes father to the thought. But here we find nothing of this wish fulfilment. As we have seen, the disciples were not expecting anything of the sort, and were reluctant to believe the evidence of their own eyes.

A fourth difficulty is this. Hallucinations tend to recur over a long period. Someone who suffers from obsessions, continues to suffer from them. But here they ceased dramatically after forty days, and were not experienced again.

And it is interesting that during the period when they did occur, they were not restricted to any particular time or place, as many such illusions are. They took place at early morning, at noon, and late at night. Seashore, roadside, upper room, garden – the locality made no difference to the appearances. Whatever these phenomena were, they were not what we understand by hallucinations. That theory will not fit the facts.

What fits the facts?

Any credible explanation must make room for three quite different pieces of evidence: the empty tomb, the resurrection appearances, and the change in the disciples. Surely a Sherlock Holmes would begin to wonder whether the Christian story was not true after all. Could it be that the body of Jesus was transmuted into a new form, vacating the tomb, appearing to the disciples, and nerving them to new endeavours? A research scientist, Dr Roger Pilkington, offers this suggestion in his fine book, *World Without End*. 'If matter is no more than an arrangement of energy, then it is perfectly conceivable (if surprising) that where the sheer essence of the whole creation was poured into human form, the body could dissociate into sheer energy and re-distil, as it were, outside the tomb, in a state which was on the average more energy than matter, but definitely material enough to have some shape and substance.' That is the way one scientist sees the probabilities of the case. It remains only one among various possibilities, but it does seem to fit the varied evidence of the New Testament accounts. It makes sense of the empty tomb, of the appearances, and of the astonishing vitality of the early Christians, who were convinced that Jesus had triumphed over man's greatest enemy, death, and that in him lay the hope of the future.

This conviction that Jesus is alive continued long after the appearances ceased. It is part of the evidence a candid investigator must look into. From that day to this Christians have claimed to *know* the risen Christ. Have they all been deluded? Are all Christians today, the world over, suffering from psychological imbalance when they lay claim to first-hand assurance that Jesus is alive? Are we to say that the whole direction given to the course of history by those eleven men in first-century Palestine is founded on an illusion? They slunk out of Jerusalem while Jesus was nailed to his cross. They went back to their homes and their fishing. Yet six weeks later they were to be found on the steps of the St Paul's Cathedral of the day, telling the clergy that they were talking nonsense, and were, moreover, guilty of judicial murder. Instead of being laughed into silence by the crowd, they won the crowd over. These Jews, with centuries of privileged pedigree behind them, threw it all away and became Christians. The whole system of Judaism was rocked to its foundations by this preaching. Does that seem likely if nothing out of the ordinary happened at Easter?

R. R. Niebuhr writes feelingly that 'those who propound the psychological theories of the resurrection of Jesus usually fail to admit the monstrous character of the interpretation of history which their theories have inevitably, if inadvertently, created'. He is quite right. Within a few years this gospel of the resurrection had spread over most of the Roman Empire. Within a generation it had reached the Imperial family. It swept the map of the ancient world. It changed the face of Roman society. The idea of resurrection was familiar enough in antiquity. It was treated in the age-old myths. It was represented by the phoenix. The ancient tombs at Byblos, thousands of years BC, show that men buried their dead in the hope of an after life, since they were interred in a sort of giant eggshell, as though they were chickens, waiting to burst forth into new life. But this was different. It was not mythology, nor hopes about the distant future. It was the actual resurrection of Jesus of Nazareth, vouched for by plenty of witnesses, that caused the stir. And this message of a risen Lord had a force for good which no hallucination has ever had. Through the risen Christ families were united after years of estrangement, immoral men became chaste and self-centred men became filled with love for other people. Wherever it has gone, this gospel has changed the characters of those who received it, and it still does. Moreover, it gives men a new joy and peace, a new zest for living, and a new concern for those less fortunate than themselves, which no humanitarian force on earth has been able to match. Some hallucination!

This, presumably, is what the resurrection appearances were designed to do. They were meant to prepare the disciples, who had known Jesus as their friend whom they could see and touch, for the future when they would know him by faith as he was spiritually with them on their mission. The appearances were not only intended to assure them of the reality of the resurrection, but to prepare them to live by faith in one they could not see, but who was none the less really their companion.

THE OLD TESTAMENT SCRIPTURES

One of the curious features in this case is the use made by the early Christians of the Old Testament. They apparently thought that the resurrection could be proved out of the Scriptures. This is understandable from one point of view: Jews believed that the truth of God was all to be found there in the Old Testament, if not in plain statement, at least in allegory or typology. So if any teaching was indeed God's truth, then it *had* to be there somewhere. From another viewpoint, however, it is very surprising indeed that they laid so much emphasis on what the Old Testament hinted about the resurrection. For, on the face of it, it said very little.

Admittedly there was that passage in Hosea which ran, 'Come, let us return to the Lord; for he has torn, that he may heal us; he has stricken, and he will bind us up. After two days he will revive us; on the third day he will raise us up, that we may live before him' (Hosea 6: 1, 2). But here the raising up means the restoring of the national fortunes, not the raising of an individual; and the 'three days' is manifestly figurative. We can be pretty sure, therefore, that it was not Scripture which 'produced' the story of the resurrection. It was the resurrection which was

49

primary for them, and they then scoured the Old Testament to find passages which might shed light on it. One passage which came nearest to expressing their convictions was Psalm 110:1, in which King David says, 'The Lord [*i.e.*, God] says to my Lord [*i.e.*, the Messiah]: "Sit at my right hand, till I make your enemies your footstool."' This had several merits. It showed that the Christ was David's 'lord' and superior, although being one of his descendants. It stressed his exaltation to God's right hand. And it looked forward to the future implications of his enthronement, the defeat of all hostile forces and the universal sovereignty of the Prince of Peace. But nobody could have read all that out of Psalm 110 if the events of that Easter week had not driven them to search the Scriptures anew.

Another of their favourite passages was to be found in Psalm 16. Here David rejoices at God's preservation from some mortal danger. He had been kept from going down to Sheol, the land of not-being. But the early Christians saw an anticipation of the resurrection of great David's greater son in the words in verse 10, 'For thou dost not give me up to Sheol, or let thy godly one see the Pit', and they backed up their interpretation of the psalm by pointing out that David could not have been talking about himself. He *did* die, and his tomb was with them, a prized national relic, to that day (Acts 2:27 ff.).

There was something radically new in this way of interpreting the Scriptures. The Christians took over all the strands in the Old Testament which gave a clue to God's coming intervention to right wrongs, and they showed that these had all reached their fulfilment in Jesus of Nazareth. Never before had ideas like the New Covenant, the Suffering Servant, the Son of Man, the Son of God, the Lord, all been used to elucidate the meaning of a historical figure. The fact that this became a commonplace in the Christian use of the Old Testament requires an epoch-making event to have triggered it off, and bespeaks a very original mind. Could it be that both the event and the mind are brought before us in the risen Jesus, who taught his disciples to see in all the Scriptures things concerning himself, and showed them that the Old Testament, rightly seen, was a Christian book? '"Everything written about me in the law of Moses and the prophets and the psalms [*i.e.*, the three divisions of the Old Testament] must be fulfilled." Then he opened their minds to understand the scriptures, and said to them, "Thus it is written, that the Christ should suffer and on the third day rise from the dead"' (Luke 24: 44 f.). Could *that* be why, as early as the ancient tradition of 1 Corinthians 15 (see page 22), the resurrection of Christ could be said to be 'according to the scriptures'?

THREE FURTHER CLUES

No good detective would leave it there. Other factors would force themselves on his attention. He would notice several things about the Christian society which are very hard to explain without the resurrection.

Sunday

These Christians met for worship on the first day of the week. They did so because it was the day on which their Lord rose from the grave: that is why they called it 'the Lord's day' (Revelation 1: 10). It was on the first day of the Jewish week that Jesus is said to have risen. Now the original Jewish rest day was Saturday. They kept that day because of the creation, when God was said to have 'rested' on the seventh day of the week, his work of creation complete. The Christians actually succeeded in changing this age-old and theologically backed day of rest. And remember, they were Jews themselves!

What chance would anyone have of doing that today, in aid of a new religion? The Seventh-Day Adventists have had a shot at moving the rest-day back to Saturday. But who takes any notice? That reminds us of the immense forces of conservatism and *laissez-faire* (above all in matters of religion) which stood in the path of these Christian innovators. It would not even have been worth trying to change it if they had not felt so strongly that the first day of the week should be set aside for the worship of the Lord who finished not the creation, but the new creation, on that day. How are we to explain the change from Saturday to Sunday worship without the resurrection?

Baptism

Then again, the Christians had an initiation ceremony. Once again they dared to clash with Judaism, this time over the traditional way of entry into the people of God, by circumcision. They said this was insufficient, indeed, irrelevant. A man must repent of his sins, believe in the risen Lord, and be baptized in water if he was to be sure of acceptance with God.

What did this baptism signify? Fortunately we are not in any doubt about that. Paul says explicitly that in baptism a man is symbolically united with Christ in his death and in his resurrection. He goes down into the water and, so to speak, dies to the old, unchanged character that he was. He rises out of the water to share a new life with the risen Christ (Romans 6: 3–5). Baptism, the initiation ceremony into world-wide Christendom, has always been linked in this way both with the death and with the resurrection of Jesus. Nothing in Christianity is older than the sacraments. How are we to account for Christian baptism, and its meaning, if the resurrection never took place?

Holy Communion

This leads on naturally to the other sacrament peculiar to Christians, the Holy Communion. This again is inexplicable without the resurrection. It was not like one of the cult feasts celebrated in contemporary paganism in honour of some dead hero of the past. It was a feast they shared with the risen Lord in exultant joy (Acts 2: 46). How could that joy have been possible if there was no resurrection? The memory of the meal which led directly to Jesus' crucifixion would have been unbearably painful for them. What transformed the anguish of the Last Supper into the joy of the Communion the world over? Surely this. They recognized the risen Lord's presence at the breaking of bread, though none of the theologians of the church throughout its centuries has been able to define that presence fully. They *met* him in this sacrament. He was not dead and gone, but risen and alive. And they would celebrate this death of his, in consciousness of his risen presence, until his longed-for return at the end of history (1 Corinthians 11:26). We possess a short eucharistic prayer from the earliest Christian community, from the original Aramaic-speaking church (1 Corinthians 16:22 and *Didache*, 10). Here it is. *Maranatha!* It means, 'Our Lord, come!' How that could have been the attitude of the early Christians as they met to celebrate the Lord's Supper among themselves is quite inexplicable, unless he did indeed rise from the dead on the third day.

REACHING A CONCLUSION

Well, what conclusion are we to reach? The evidence on the scene of the crucifixion and burial, the changed lives of the disciples, the appearances, the claim throughout nineteen centuries that Jesus is a living reality (together with transformed characters to back up that claim) all drive us to conclude that Jesus did rise that third day. The appeal to Scripture, the sacraments of Communion and Baptism and the change in the day of rest all point in the same direction. This evidence was sufficient to convince leading Jewish intellectuals of the calibre of Paul of Tarsus, and leading Roman politicians like Sergius Paulus, Governor of Cyprus. Hard though it may be to believe, any alternative suggestion is even harder to credit. The evidence points unmistakably to the fact that on the third day Jesus rose.

This was the conclusion to which a former Lord Chief Justice of England, Lord Darling, came. At a private dinner party the talk turned to the truth of Christianity, and particularly to a certain book dealing with the resurrection. Placing his fingertips together, assuming a judicial attitude, and speaking with a quiet emphasis that was extraordinarily impressive, he said, 'We, as Christians, are asked to take a very great deal on trust; the teachings, for example, and the miracles of Jesus. If we had to take all on trust, I, for one, should be sceptical. The crux of the problem of whether Jesus was, or was not, what he proclaimed himself to be, must surely depend upon the truth or otherwise of the resurrection. On that greatest point we are not merely asked to have faith. In its favour as a living truth there exists such overwhelming evidence, positive and negative, factual and circumstantial, that no intelligent jury in the world could fail to bring in a verdict that the resurrection story is true.'

Do you feel that goes too far? If so, why not carry out an investigation on your own? Take the accounts in the four Gospels and 1 Corinthians 15 and see if you can adequately explain them on any other hypothesis. No alternative solution has ever won much acceptance yet. The most recent attempt, by Hugh Schonfield, to which we have already referred (p. 33), is pathetically thin. It does not begin to make sense of the phenomena, least of all of the amazing change in the disciples. He does not even seem to have convinced himself of the plausibility of his 'Passover Plot' in which, he suggests, Jesus was drugged and survived his ordeal in the tomb long enough to say a few words to his rescuers before expiring. For he concludes, rather lamely, 'There is room for other theories, such as that the man concerned [i.e., in first announcing the resurrection] was a medium, and that Jesus, risen from the dead into the After Life in the Spiritualist sense, spoke through him in his own voice, which enabled his presence to be recognized.' Not very impressive, is it?

Compare it with a thorough-going examination of the evidence by a thoughtful lawyer who did not believe in the resurrection when he began his enquiry. In what has become a best-seller, *Who Moved the Stone?*, Frank Morison tells us how he had been brought up in a rationalistic environment, and had come to the opinion that the resurrection was nothing but a fairy-tale happy ending which spoiled the matchless story of Jesus. Accordingly, he planned to write an account of the last tragic days of

Jesus, allowing the full horror of the crime and the full heroism of Jesus to shine through. He would, of course, omit any suspicion of the miraculous, and would utterly discount the resurrection. But when he came to study the facts with care, he had to change his mind, and he wrote his book on the other side. His first chapter is significantly called, 'The Book that Refused to be Written', and the rest of his volume consists of one of the shrewdest and most attractively written assessments I have ever read of the evidence which demonstrates the truth of the resurrection.

It is well worth taking the trouble to examine the matter carefully for yourself. For Christianity does not hold the resurrection to be one among many tenets of belief. Without faith in the resurrection *there would be no Christianity at all*. The Christian church would never have begun; the Jesus-movement would have fizzled out like a damp squib with his execution. Christianity stands or falls with the truth of the resurrection. Once disprove it, and you have disposed of Christianity.

This was realized in the pleasure-seeking, cynical days of the eighteenth century, when unbelief was as fashionable as it is today. The Frenchman, Montesquieu, made this comment about eighteenth-century religion in Britain, 'In England there is no religion, and the subject, if mentioned in Society, excites nothing but laughter'.

Bishop Butler, the philosopher, writing at the same time, commented, 'It has come to be taken for granted that Christianity is not so much a subject for enquiry but that it is now at length discovered to be fictitious.' It was against this background that two able young men, Gilbert West and Lord Lyttleton, went up to Oxford. They were friends of Dr Johnson and Alexander Pope, in the swim of society. They were determined to attack the very basis of the Christian faith. So Lyttleton settled down to prove that Saul of Tarsus was never converted to Christianity, and West to demonstrate that Jesus never rose from the tomb.

Some time later, they met to discuss their findings. Both were a little sheepish. For they had come independently to similar and disturbing conclusions. Lyttleton found, on examination, that Saul of Tarsus *did* become a radically new man through his conversion to Christianity; and West found that the evidence pointed unmistakably to the fact that Jesus did rise from the dead. You may still find his book in a large library. It is entitled *Observations on the History and Evidences of the Resurrection of Jesus Christ*, and was published in 1747. On the fly-leaf he has had printed this telling quotation from Ecclesiasticus 11 : 7, which might be adopted with profit by any modern agnostic: *'Blame not before thou hast examined the truth.'*

Examine the resurrection for yourself. It can stand any amount of honest scrutiny, for the simple reason that it is the truth. The man is alive!

CHAPTER FIVE

DOES IT MATTER?

DOES IT REALLY MATTER whether Jesus rose from the dead or not? What difference can a matter of ancient history like that make to a busy modern man, who has time to consider religious ideas only if they are both important in themselves and relevant to daily life? Surely people are not asking, 'Did Jesus rise from the dead?', but much broader questions like the following: 'Is there a God?', 'Are all religions of equal value?' and 'What happens after death?'

These are indeed questions of vital importance, but there is not much sign that we are getting nearer to agreed answers to them. Could it be that we are looking in the wrong direction? Is it possible that in the resurrection of Jesus of Nazareth we have the clue to these queries which are so often aired these days? If so, there will be no further doubts about whether the resurrection matters or not. It will come into its own as the master-key to unlock these three intractable locks. I believe that the resurrection is the proper starting-point if we are to find our way through the maze of muddled thinking on these questions. Let us look at them in turn.

IS THERE A GOD?

I am constantly astonished to see arguments continuing to pass to and fro, even in learned journals like *Mind*, purporting to prove or disprove the existence of God. The whole procedure is ludicrous because, although there are good reasons for believing in a Supreme Being, personal existence can neither be proved nor disproved. It must be encountered. And the only God of which the Bible knows anything is not the First Cause or the Unmoved Mover discussed in philosophical argument, but the living God who made man, who cares for him, and who comes to meet him in Jesus Christ. It is therefore beside the point when a man like Bertrand Russell wastes so much powder and shot in *Why I am not a Christian* refuting the traditional intellectual arguments for the existence of God. The Bible never uses them. It never argues about God's existence at all – but always assumes it. It points, instead, to Jesus Christ who revealed God to us. This claim is enough to make the imagination boggle. It means that behind this world there is a loving, personal Creator God. This God cares for us men so much, despite our waywardness and rebellion, that he chose to come and share our world, and to make known to us his nature and his will in the only terms we ultimately understand, the terms of a human life.

And what a life! A life that has influenced art, music, literature and culture generally, more than any other before or since. A life which has inspired the ideals of modern education, hospitals, social services, freedom, the trade unions and the welfare state. A life which embodied every virtue known to man, and was free from all human vices. However you look at it, the character of Jesus was

57

unique. He set the highest standards for human conduct that any teacher has ever set, and, unlike any other man, he kept those standards.

Not only is the life of Jesus admired outside Christian circles; so is his teaching. Thus Lord Boothby can say, in the midst of launching a scathing assault on Christianity in the collection of essays entitled *What I Believe*, 'I believe the teachings of Jesus are the best that have been offered to mankind'. As a self-confessed atheist he thinks that when he has paid tribute to the life and teaching of Jesus, that is the end of the matter. But he is greatly mistaken. He has either gone too far or not far enough.

For this wonderful man Jesus made the most shattering claims in the course of this teaching of his. There is no parallel to them in any of the world's religions. And it simply will not do to neglect them, as is commonly done by agnostic writers. Yet if you accept them as part of the authentic record about Jesus that has come down to us, then at once the cosy picture of Jesus as merely a good man and a great teacher disintegrates. As C. S. Lewis in his *Miracles* crisply expressed it, 'The discrepancy between the depth and sanity, and (let me add) *shrewdness* of his moral teaching, and the rampant megalomania which must lie behind his theological teaching unless he is indeed God, has never been satisfactorily got over.' For Jesus claimed to be authorized by God to forgive sins (Mark 2 : 5; Luke 7 : 48), to give life (John 6 : 35; 10 : 28; 11 : 25), to raise men from the dead at the last day (John 5 : 27–29), and to be the final judge of all mankind (Matthew 25 : 31 ff.; John 5 : 22). Imagine a modern religious leader saying that the eternal destiny of his hearers depended upon their obedience to him. 'Such a preacher', as J. R. W. Stott pertinently observes in *Basic Christianity*, 'would not long escape the attentions of the police or the psychiatrists.'

Moreover, Jesus accepted as his due the worship thought proper to God alone. Peter fell at his feet and said, 'You are the Christ, the Son of the living God' (Matthew 16 : 16). Again Thomas, in the upper room, cried out, 'My Lord and my God!' (John 20 : 28). In both instances Jesus accepted such tributes quite naturally. Did he rebuke Thomas for his enthusiastic outburst? Not in the least— except for not having believed it earlier! Now no good man would behave like that. The Acts of the Apostles tells how both Peter and Paul found simple people who wanted to worship them, and they both recoiled in horror at the thought. Not so Jesus. He took it as his right.

Claims such as this are breathtaking. They would sound like the ravings of a lunatic were it not for the character of the man who uttered them, and for the quality of the teaching he brought. But how did he propose to authenticate his claims? Not by miracles. He refused to work these to order. They could never compel belief: men would always find some alternative explanation. He made his position perfectly plain in Matthew 12:39, 40. Here he told his hearers that no sign would be given them to validate his claims, except the sign of the prophet Jonah. And what was that? Well, as every child knows, Jonah was the man who spent three days inside the great fish. Similarly Jesus said he would spend three days buried in the heart of the earth. That would be the demonstration that he spoke the truth. He continued, 'At the Judgement, when this generation is on trial, the men of Nineveh will appear against it and ensure its condemnation, for they repented at the preaching of Jonah; and what is here is greater than Jonah' (Matthew 12:41, NEB). Jesus was as good as his word. His resurrection after three days in the heart of the earth did indeed authenticate his claim.

A Ugandan friend of mine sees this clearly. 'For me, he is not a mere human hero of history, like those who fought and died in two World Wars. He is my God, in full power of deity.' That is what Paul meant when he wrote, 'He was declared Son of God by a mighty act in that he rose from the dead' (Romans 1:4, NEB). The most compelling argument for the existence of God is Jesus Christ. By his incarnation, his teaching, his death and resurrection he has shown us what God is like. He shows us that God is personal. He shows us that God is holy. He shows us that God is love. He shows us that God forgives—at infinite personal cost. He shows us, by the resurrection, that evil will not have the last word in God's universe. In the risen Christ we have the answer to our doubts about God. That is why the resurrection matters.

WHICH RELIGION?

When the subject of religion is broached, many people take refuge from personal involvement by saying, 'Well, which religion shall it be? There are so many.' As a rule this attitude is frivolous, and is an excuse for not taking part in any religion. Many people who make this sort of remark have, in any case, no knowledge of other religions. If they had, they would think again. What religion in the world, apart from the Judaeo-Christian faith, is intellectually coherent, morally dynamic, and big enough to embrace life and death, creation and redemption, the individual whatever his race or class, and the community as well? But for those seriously troubled by the variety of religions in the world, the resurrection may well prove the most useful and secure starting-point.

There is all the world of difference between the resuscitation of a corpse and the resurrection of Jesus Christ. Christians are most certainly not asserting that a certain man died a couple of thousand years ago, was brought back to life again for a while, and then died for good and all. No. They are saying that Almighty God took our human nature, that he died, that he rose again victorious over death, never more to die. 'We know that Christ being raised from the dead will never die again; death no longer has dominion over him' (Romans 6:9). His resurrection says 'Yes' to his claims to be the Way, the Truth, the Life. It was not just any old person who rose. It was *this man*. And the resurrection vindicated his claims to deity.

This therefore is the place to begin. Do not waste a lot of time investigating every religion under the sun from Animism to Hinduism. Examine the evidence for the resurrection of Jesus Christ instead. If he is risen, you need look no further.

You will, of course, find much to admire, much to learn

from, in other religions (as well as a lot of filth and cruelty): God has not left himself without witness throughout his world. But you will not find in them anything that is good and true which cannot be found in Christianity. Nowhere else will you find out about a God who cares for you enough to die for you, to rise from the grave as a pledge of your future, and to be willing to come and actually share your life with you. Nowhere else will you find a religion that meets your needs in that radical and intimate way. If Jesus did rise from the dead, then he is the Way to God (John 14:6). In that case, the exclusiveness of the Christian claim makes sense. It is not that Christians are narrow-minded or uncharitable about other faiths. But if Jesus is indeed, as the resurrection asserts, God himself come to our rescue, then to reject him, or even to neglect him, is ultimate folly. That is why Jesus is not, and never can be, just one among the many religious leaders of the world. He is not even the best. He is the only. Among various examples of the relative, he stands out as the Absolute. In the risen Jesus, God Almighty confronts us with shattering directness. He offers us total succour; but he demands from us total allegiance. It is splendid to have an interest in comparative religion. But the more you know of the others, the more clearly Christianity is seen to be unique. And the key to Christianity is the resurrection.

Christianity is a historical religion. It claims that God has taken the risk of involving himself in human history, and the facts are there for you to examine with the utmost rigour. They will stand any amount of critical investigation: indeed, no book on earth has been subjected to such prolonged and intense scrutiny by some of the best minds in the world over many hundreds of years as the New Testament. Of course, there are plenty of people who scoff at the Christian position, but unfortunately one generally finds that they have not taken the trouble to study it carefully at first hand. Second-hand opinions are worthless on a matter of this importance, where the stakes are so high. You must satisfy yourself by looking into the matter. But if you conclude that Jesus Christ did rise from

61

the tomb, then for you that settles the question of other religions. Christ can no longer appear to you as the finest of men. Although completely human, he is nothing less than God. And as God he claims your loyal obedience.

This point is well made by the famous meeting of Auguste Comte, the French philosopher, and Thomas Carlyle. Comte said he intended to found a new religion, which would sweep away Christianity and everything else. He was enthusiastic about it. Carlyle's devastating reply ran something like this. 'Splendid. All you need to do is to speak as never man spoke, to live as never man lived, to be crucified, rise again the third day, and get the world to believe you are still alive. Then your religion will have some chance of success.'

WHAT HAPPENS AFTER DEATH?

A few years ago *The Sunday Times* ran a series of articles in which distinguished men gave their ideas of what would happen after death. There was Christmas Humphreys the Buddhist, Lord Dowding the Spiritualist, Basil Henriques the Jew, Bertrand Russell the atheist, and so on. The articles aroused a lot of interest, and were published as a book, *The Great Mystery of Life Hereafter*. The somewhat motley collection of views brought together in this way showed several things: that man is fascinated by this problem; that there is a general belief (even among rationalists) in some sort of survival; and that there is a most bewildering difference of opinion on the matter. One view is as good as another: nobody knows for sure, for the very good reason that nobody has experienced death and come back to tell us what it is like. It seems that we are reduced to guesswork: we can never get any certain knowledge.

It seemed like that in the late Middle Ages over a very different matter, the possibility of a sea route to India. There was a great deal of speculation about this in political and economic circles in European capitals. Was there a way to the rich land of spices round the southern tip of Africa? Nobody could be quite sure, though many suspected that there was. All attempts to round the Cape had failed. So much so that this treacherous headland where the Atlantic and Indian Oceans meet was known as the Cape of Storms, and it was the scene of many a wreck. However, one intrepid mariner determined to try again. At length he succeeded in rounding the Cape and reaching the East. There is still a monument to this famous sailor, Vasco da Gama, in China today. Ever since he sailed back in triumph to Lisbon it has become impossible to doubt that a way to the Orient does exist round the bottom of Africa. The very name of that terrible Cape was changed to its present title, the Cape of Good Hope.

The enigma of life after death is rather like that. Up to the time when Jesus died and rose again, death was like that Cape of Storms, littered with wrecks. Until his successful rounding of that Cape and return, men had nothing to go on but speculation about the after life. His resurrection has turned it into the Cape of Good Hope. He has opened up for his people the way to a new and rich land which he has shown exists. And because he has satisfactorily rounded that perilous Cape, he is well equipped to act as pilot to others. Christian optimism about the future life is, accordingly, not (as Bertrand Russell in his *Sunday Times* article complained) 'built on the ground that fairy-tales are pleasant', but founded on the solid basis of the resurrection of Jesus Christ from the grave. And he promised his followers that he would go to prepare a place for them, so that where he was, they might be also (John 14: 2, 3).

'He has', wrote C. S. Lewis in his book *Miracles*, 'forced open a door that had been locked since the death of the first man. He has met, fought, and beaten the King of Death. Everything is different because He has done so. This is the beginning of the New Creation: a new chapter in cosmic history has opened.'

If you want an answer, supported by solid evidence, to three of the most baffling questions a man can ask (and does ask, very frequently), then it is the resurrection of Jesus Christ that provides the clue. We are constantly told the importance of asking the right questions; but the trouble is that in religious matters we do not know what the right questions are. So we pose those disconnected queries about the existence of God, the different religions, and life after death. But the Bible does not encourage us to ask these questions at all. To do so is to court inconclusive and unsatisfactory answers. The Bible urges us to make up our minds about Jesus of Nazareth and his resurrection. When we begin with the solid facts and clear evidence which can lead us to a positive conclusion about him, then we shall be in a position to answer those other questions that spring more immediately to our minds. The resurrection shows us that there is a God, that Jesus Christ is the way to God, and that death for the Christian leads into the nearer presence of God. That is why the resurrection matters.

CHAPTER SIX

A LIFE WORTH LIVING

WHEN THE EARLY CHRISTIANS began preaching to such great effect about Jesus and the resurrection, they were impelled by two main considerations. Firstly, it was *true*: Jesus had risen from that grave. And secondly, it was *relevant*: the risen Christ was transforming men's lives. These are the two reasons that have impelled the writing of this book. In the last three chapters we have concentrated for the most part on the truth of the resurrection. For the next three I propose to look more carefully into its relevance.

Anybody in thoughtful mood will admit that there are various things which spoil life, things which stop us living life to the full and limit our satisfaction. Christians claim that the resurrection of Jesus makes a real difference to these frustrations which everybody experiences. The resurrection impinges on five areas of depression, so to speak, which afflict us all from time to time. It touches our sense of guilt, of inadequacy, of discontent, of lostness and of loneliness.

THE SENSE OF GUILT

We all know what it is to feel bad about something we have done. It may have been a piece of flagrant deception, it may have been a bitter retort, it may have been an exhibition of greed or lust or temper. Whatever it was, we feel thoroughly ashamed of ourselves. Admittedly, we do not think like this very often; there is no point in it, for there is nothing we can do about the past. Yet we have, at times, an uneasy conscience: and we cannot, in all honesty, enter a plea of 'diminished responsibility' on our own behalf. Indeed, the Bible does not conceal the fact that we are guilty, genuinely morally responsible to a holy God whom we have affronted, whether we *feel* guilty or not. Our problem is not so much guilt-feelings (for which there may be psychological explanations) as real guilt: we are all in the wrong with God.

The New Testament makes it very plain that Jesus Christ came into the world to deal with this predicament of ours. That is why he died upon the cross, an event so central to his whole life that nearly a half of the Gospel story is devoted to it. He had come to settle our debts for us, and to rectify this sinful bias in our nature. This was the most difficult and the most costly enterprise that has ever been undertaken in the history of the world.

John the Baptist hailed Jesus as the Lamb of God who would take away (or perhaps, take upon himself) the sin of the world (John 1:29). That would have made the Jews sit up. They knew all about lambs that took away sin. Their sacrificial system was a constant reminder of the awful results of wrongdoing: the innocent lamb died in order that the offender might live on. This was the heart of Israelite religion. Yet it had not satisfied some of her finest minds. There were prophets and psalmists of Israel who were well aware that the death of a dumb animal could not alter the moral state of a responsible and free human being.

And so the highest conception of sin and forgiveness to be found in the whole of the Old Testament is expressed in that famous chapter, Isaiah 53.

Here some majestic, mysterious sufferer accepts responsibility for the sins of the people. 'All we like sheep have gone astray; we have turned every one to his own way; and the Lord has laid on him the iniquity of us all.'

It was a voluntary death: 'he poured out his soul to death, and was numbered with the transgressors; yet he bore the sin of many, and made intercession for the transgressors.'

It was a ghastly death: 'He was despised and rejected by men; a man of sorrows, and acquainted with grief; and as one from whom men hide their faces he was despised, and we esteemed him not.'

It was a vicarious death: 'surely he has borne our griefs and carried our sorrows; yet we esteemed him stricken, smitten by God, and afflicted. But he was wounded for our transgressions, he was bruised for our iniquities; upon him was the chastisement that made us whole, and with his stripes we are healed.'

Now Jesus quite explicitly applied this ancient prophecy to himself. And it fitted wonderfully well, even down to the details. There is, of course, no question of Jesus trying to 'fix' his death in accordance with the prophecy – the manner of one's death is something it is very difficult to organize exactly! But the fulfilment of Isaiah's words, 'And they made his grave with the wicked and with a rich man in his death, although he had done no violence' is very striking. For, of course, Jesus did die alongside two *wicked* men, *although he had done no violence*, and he was buried in the loaned tomb of Joseph, *a rich man*. This is merely one of the details that fits into place once you see Jesus' death on the cross as the fulfilment of this prophecy. He was the Lamb dying for the guilty party; he was the Suffering Servant of the Lord taking responsibility for the sins of the world. That is the essence of the Christian gospel. But at the very core of this good news there is a

66

question-mark. Did his death suffice? Was the cry, 'It is finished', which he uttered as he died, a shout of triumph or of despair? Did he vanquish the forces of evil, or did they crush him?

We could never know, if it were not for the resurrection. The fact that Jesus rose again is the assurance we have that he did cope with that load on our behalf, he did win that titanic struggle. That is why St Paul wrote, he 'was put to death for our trespasses and raised for our justification' (Romans 4: 25). Did Jesus die and rise again? Then I can be sure his sacrifice was sufficient, I can know that my acquittal is assured and that my past is forgiven. For on that cross he shouldered my burden, and underwrote my debts – and to prove it, *he rose again*.

I shall never forget the joy on the face of a student when he understood this truth. He had been burdened by a sense of his past guilty deeds, and had, in fact, written down an enormous list of them and brought it with him. As he saw what Jesus had done for him on the cross, and how this was guaranteed by the resurrection, he began to find a peace he had not known before: Christ had done for him what he could not do for himself. Together we tore up that list of failures!

All down the ages men have found in the cross and resurrection of Jesus a remedy for their sense of guilt. John Bunyan expressed it in this picturesque way in his classic, *Pilgrim's Progress*.

'He ran thus till he came to a place somewhat ascending; and upon that place stood a cross, and a little below in the bottom, a sepulchre. So I saw in my dream, that just as Christian came up with the cross, his burden loosed from off his shoulders, and fell from his back; and began to tumble; and so continued to do, till it came to the mouth of the sepulchre, where it fell in, and I saw it no more.

'Then was Christian glad and lightsome, and said with a merry heart, "He hath given me rest, by his sorrow, and life, by his death." . . . Then Christian gave three leaps for joy, and went on singing.'

That is how it appeared to John Bunyan 300 years ago

in Bedford prison. This is how it appears to Michael Alison, a present-day Member of Parliament in Westminster. 'My conviction about the certainty of the resurrection is based upon the profound sense of forgiveness which I enjoy. This in turn springs from the spiritual (and no doubt, psychological) relief and freedom I find in being able to dissociate myself from the dark deeds I have done or might do, and associating them with the dead and mutilated Christ. My "old self" is, in a way I can actually experience with inward conviction, done away with, and destroyed in Christ.

'Yet it goes without saying that the experience of peace and liberation this transference brings, would be inconceivable without the actuality of a living fellowship with the risen Jesus. For the profoundest element in my fellowship with God, the deepest sense I have of his omnipotence, lies precisely in this: that he can allow himself to be destroyed by the worst that is in me, and yet can come back loving! Without the actual fellowship of loving God in Christ, the past transference of guilt would be a mere expediency, a cause for deepening, not relieving, self-centredness and remorse.'

THE SENSE OF INADEQUACY

It is not only our sense of shame about the past which troubles us from time to time. Much more pressing for most of us is our chronic failure to be able to turn over a new leaf. We try to reform ourselves, but it rarely works for long. An atheist undergraduate friend once wrote to me like this: 'Why do I need God to help me control my faults? Shouldn't I rather strive to better myself? I've tried that for a year now, and succeeded mostly, except when during exams I was very bitter and twisted. I've tried to excuse this, but I can't. I should be able to control myself at all times. So I'll try harder!' All credit to her for trying, but it was not a success. Some six months later I got another letter with this revealing comment, 'I feel so selfish always working and slaving only for myself, and even though I swore I could, in the old days, force myself to become a much nicer person, all through will power, I find I can't. I'm too lazy, and I never get round to it.' That is a very honest admission, and I suspect we have all had the same experience.

It is this sense of inadequacy to make ourselves better people that the risen Christ can alter. He offers, as we have seen, to come and share life with us, and indeed to take up residence within us, so that, to quote St Paul, his strength is made perfect in our weakness (2 Corinthians 12:9). This is exactly what the earliest believers in the risen Lord discovered. Paul himself might have been discouraged, resentful and lonely as he lay in prison for his faith. Instead he wrote: 'I wish you all joy in the Lord. I will say it again: all joy be yours. . . . The Lord is near; have no anxiety, but in everything make your requests known to God. . . . Then the peace of God, which is beyond our utmost understanding, will keep guard over your hearts and thoughts, in Christ Jesus. . . . I know what it is to be brought low, and I know what it is to have plenty. I have been very thoroughly initiated into the human lot with all its ups and downs – fullness and hunger, plenty and want. *I have strength for anything through him who gives me power*' (Philippians 4: 4, 6, 7, 12 f., NEB).

That is what the resurrection meant to Paul: strength for anything through him who gave him power. As he expressed it with great vividness on another occasion, the resurrection means that the very power of God which raised Christ from the tomb is available to raise us from the rut of our own failures (Ephesians 1: 19 f.). Did it work for the ordinary run of Christians in New Testament times, as well as for saints like Paul? Indeed it did. We have already had occasion to notice the remarkable change in the morals of the Corinthians after their conversion to Christ (p. 21). The same is true of the Ephesians. They had been pagans, immoral, callous, abandoned. 'But that', says the apostle, 'is not how you learned Christ.' He reminds them in Ephesians 4: 20 ff. (NEB) that when they received God's Holy Spirit into their lives they said farewell to 'that old human nature which, deluded by its lusts, is sinking towards death'. They had 'put on the new nature of God's creating, which shows itself in the just and devout life called for by the truth'. And what did that mean in ordinary everyday conduct? 'Throw off falsehood; speak the truth to each other, for all of us are the parts of one body. If you are angry, do not let anger lead you into sin; do not let sunset find you still nursing it; leave no loop-hole for the devil. The thief must give up stealing, and instead work hard and honestly with his own hands, so that he may have something to share with the needy.' Just pause for a moment to consider the revolution in values that lies behind that statement. The philosophy of 'Get by any means' has been driven out by the love of Christ which impels a man to 'Give to anyone in need'.

It would be useful to follow Paul through the fourth and fifth chapters of Ephesians, and see how all these practical exhortations to a new sort of life spring from letting 'the Holy Spirit fill you' (Ephesians 5: 18, NEB). But enough has been said to show the great difference in ordinary men and women, won from first-century paganism by the message of a risen Saviour who could deliver them from themselves.

It is no less true today. Let us return to the MP I quoted previously, Michael Alison. 'The base and pagan in me struggle continually to gain recognition as the essential me; but in spite of securing isolated successes, they cannot displace the fundamental consciousness of the power and love of a greater force from outside which has possessed me.'

Or, as a man bedridden with an incurable disease wrote, 'Christ has made it possible to accept suffering without inner resentment, bitterness or boredom. Those are the burdens he has taken from me. He has given me in return peace of heart, joy and illumination during the lonely hours, and a focus of attention always away from myself, because there is so much work to be done for him even when I'm flat out on my back.'

The atheist to whom I referred on page 68 has written to tell me that after two years of reasoning, struggling and trying to find satisfactory alternatives, she has become a Christian. In the end, it was the loving lives of a Christian couple which precipitated the crisis of her own personal commitment. 'Their love of God and of each other so filled the whole home that it fairly hit one in the face as one entered the house. This made me finally realize the difference between Christians and others – it changes their lives so much.' And what difference did it make to her when she took this step of commitment? One thing was a deep joy and peace, 'the greatest joy I have ever known'. Another was a growing transformation of character: 'I find I have the strength to do so many things I've been too apathetic to do before, and just as I'm about to scream with rage at someone, or say something unkind, I find I have the will-power not to. My mother says I'm so gentle all of a sudden – she can't get over it.' There is no touch of smugness here, for she continues, 'I'm beginning to realize just what a beastly person I am – so full of pride that I despair of ever being humble.' But there is the authentic Christian conviction, based on first-hand experience, of what God can do to make new men of us: 'I know that with God's help I can become a much nicer person than I am, and can realize some of the high ideals I've always had but never done much about.'

Jesus once said, 'Every one who commits sin is a slave to sin . . . So if the Son makes you free, you will be free indeed' (John 8: 34, 36). He means us to know in our own experience the liberating power his risen life can bring. And that is as possible in our own day as it was in the first century AD.

THE SENSE OF DISCONTENT

One of the characteristic marks of contemporary Western society is, as we noted in Chapter One, that although we have so many material advantages, we are not conspicuously happy. There is a disenchantment, a discontent about many people's lives for much of the time. We are taken aback when we meet someone who is habitually and radiantly happy. But it is that sort of happiness which Jesus Christ offers to the Christian. I do not know where the idea sprang from that Christians are miserable. It is certainly false. Jesus promised his followers that he would give them his own joy, a joy which nobody and nothing would be able to take from them (John 15:11; 16:22). This is, after all, what one would expect. When a man is reconciled with his Maker, living as God intended him to live, and sharing his experiences with the risen Christ, it is not surprising that he should be happy.

Yona Kanamuzeyi was a devoted African pastor. On 23 January, 1964, he was martyred in the Ruanda riots. He was carried off from his home, shot in the back, and then pushed into the river. Before he died, he prayed for his executioners, and then, so an eyewitness records, went to his death joyfully singing a hymn. The soldiers were all amazed. They had never before seen a man walking calmly and unafraid to meet his murderers as he did, like a man taking an afternoon stroll. The companionship of the risen Christ gave him a poise and a contentment which death itself could not destroy. Was it not this sort of thing that Paul had in mind when he wrote that lyrical passage at the end of the eighth chapter of Romans? 'As Scripture says: "we have been treated like sheep for slaughter" – and yet, in spite of all, overwhelming victory is ours through him who loved us. For I am convinced that there is nothing in death or life, in the realm of spirits or super-human powers, in the world as it is or the world as it shall be . . . – nothing in all creation that can separate us from the love of God in Christ our Lord' (Romans 8:36–39, NEB). Christians down the ages have proved the truth of that conviction.

A very different example of true Christian contentment reached me only this morning. One of our students, train-ing for ordination at the London College of Divinity, hitched a lift with a Birmingham lorry driver. No sooner was he in the cab, than the man began to speak to him about Jesus Christ, not knowing, of course, that he too was a Christian. He said, 'I've been driving for twenty-eight years, and I love every moment of it, because I do it for God. I pray as I'm unloading, and sing as I'm driving.' There was a man who was experiencing the joy that is his birthright as a Christian. When Jesus said, 'No one will take your joy from you' (John 16: 22), he meant it.

There is nothing synthetic about this Christian contentment. It persists even in the most unpleasant circumstances. A friend of mine has recently had to go into a mental hospital. She is a Christian, and in the midst of trying circumstances has been trying to help others there. She has gone out of her way to be of service to an old, senile woman. One day this old lady asked her what made her different from the rest of the patients. She replied, 'Perhaps it is that I am determined to get right and to get out of here.' The old woman persisted, 'No, there's more to it than that, isn't there?' 'Yes, there is more to it than that,' admitted my friend shyly (she does not find it easy to talk about her faith). 'You see, I love Jesus. That is what makes the difference.'

Another friend of mine and his wife have come to a living Christian faith in the past two or three years. Things have certainly not gone easily for them. One of their children became dangerously ill, and there was little hope of her recovery. The business he was in became bankrupt, and he had to look for another job in a hurry. It seemed that they would have to give up their home. What were they to do? 'In our weakness', he writes, 'we found that tremendous strength and peace of mind from God which we had heard about. Of course, we prayed and prayed, and in an almost frightening way our prayers were answered, almost by return of post! I well remember saying to a friend, "With God on your side you just can't lose".'

The composure of this couple in their distress was very remarkable. It can only be explained by their daily companionship with the risen Lord who gave them his peace throughout it all. Indeed they have turned into one of the most consistently joyful Christian couples I know. It so happens that their daughter's health has wonderfully improved, a new job (at a considerably lower salary) has turned up, and they have not had to leave their home –

you might call this a happy ending. But the experience has burnt in upon them a deep understanding of God's care and protection, his power and peace in a period of great crisis, and you can see this in their faces and in their attitudes. Financially much poorer now, they have the incalculable riches of inner happiness which springs from their relationship with their living Lord. Discontent has given way to gratitude and joy.

THE SENSE OF LOSTNESS

Our generation certainly knows what it is to be lost. No overriding aim in life, no enduring relationships, no deep satisfaction. This feeling of lostness is well brought out in John Lennon and Paul McCartney's song, *The Nowhere Man*.

'He's a real nowhere man
Sitting in his nowhere land
Making all his nowhere plans for nobody.

Doesn't have a point of view,
Knows not where he's going to –
Isn't he a bit like me and you?

This is one of the areas of life where Jesus Christ makes a most striking difference. He builds up lasting relationships between those who belong to him, however incompatible they were by nature. The New Testament does not only say that the bodies of individual Christians constitute the temples in which the Holy Spirit of the risen Lord comes to live, wonderful though that is. It also makes clear that the Christian community as a whole is the shrine that the Lord inhabits. God brings together in the closest harmony in his temple stones and bricks that would otherwise never have been anywhere near each other. I well remember one person at school I simply could not stand. He felt just the same about me. It so happened that I came first to a personal faith in Christ. And I gradually found my attitude towards him changing. Then he too became a

74

Christian, and we found that we not only got on well together, but became close friends. That example has stuck in my mind, because it was the first time I had seen the Lord knitting two otherwise incompatible people together in a relationship of real love. But I have witnessed it hundreds of times since, in several countries of the world, among Christians black, white, and coloured. In an age that knows what it means to be lost, and has seen the breakdown of personal relationships on an unprecedented scale, one of the most precious things about Christianity is the fellowship forged by the Lord between those who belong to him. It is to my mind one of the strongest evidences of the truth of Christianity.

Our lostness does not include only the breakdown of relationships, but the lack of purpose so noticeable today. The ex-pop star, Terry Dene, is a good example of what I mean. Here was a young man who achieved great success. He performed before millions on TV, and appeared in shows in all the major cities of England. But he was dissatisfied, and shiftless. He became violent and destructive. He was overcome by mental depression. He parted from his wife. 'I drifted more and more into the pit of despair,' he wrote. 'I gave up hope of ever becoming anything in life. Psychiatrists, doctors all tried to help me, but to no avail. There was no last straw to cling to.' That man is now a Christian, working with the Mobile Evangelistic Crusade, through which he came to Christ. He knows from experience that Jesus came 'to seek and to save the lost'. 'Today I am far from the bright lights and glamour, but I am truly happier than I have ever been. Many young people desire fame, prestige, clothes and money. But none of these satisfy. I know. I've had them all in abundance, and from my own hard experience I can honestly say that nothing, nothing at all, can compare with the joy of knowing Jesus and being at peace with God.'

One of the consequences of this new sense of community and of personal integration is that Christians become keen to share their faith with others, in order that they too may find a life worth living. One man I know often chats quite naturally about his Lord with beatniks, people in the bus or in the coffee bar. The joy of the Lord is very much in evidence in his life. I asked him to give me an example of the difference the love of Christ has made to his attitude to others, and he wrote this. 'I think of that ragged old woman, smelly, raving, an outcast of society, whom I met near Charing Cross at one of our open-air services. I could never have gone up to her of my own accord, brought her a cup of tea and tried to be of some help, were it not that Christ living in me impelled me to do so, despite the laughs and jeers of the onlookers. Because he is alive, I want to share him with others.'

It is this experience of the living Lord that is the main-spring of Christian action. It inspired the Wilberforces and Shaftesburys of a former day, and it still does. Thus it is well known among the 'gentlemen of the road' that if you want real care and a chance to get rehabilitated, you do not usually go to one of the secular institutions for the destitute, but rather to a Christian place like the crypt of St George's, Leeds, or of Christ Church, Spitalfields. The doctors, clergy, cooks and social workers there really care for these tramps because they are filled with the love of Christ.

Not long ago *The Weekend Telegraph* published an article about Charles Preece, who runs a home, Wayfarer House, for ex-prisoners, alcoholics, and meths drinkers off the nearby bomb-site. Why does he bother? Because he came face to face with the living Christ at a Billy Graham meeting in Glasgow, in March 1955. That is why. The love of Christ drove him to want 'to do something which was more help to my fellow-men than being in business', so he became a full-time Welfare Officer, working among these outcasts of society. He does not push religion in Wayfarer House. As a Christian man he offers his visitors friendship; for that is what the risen Christ has offered him.

THE SENSE OF LONELINESS

On 2 June, 1966, *The Sun* featured the one-man exhibi-tion by the famous artist, Annigoni. He was asked, 'Which picture would you like to be remembered by?' and he replied, 'Solitude'. He was so impressed by the loneliness of modern man that he has painted no less than twelve pictures on this subject. In one of them, life-size nuns, bishops and priests flee from some unseen terror. 'The church', Annigoni explained, 'in trying to accommodate to this present century, is failing badly. The only way it can succeed is to go right back to Christ. This is what the picture is about. The priests are like sheep; they are just running with their heads down. The nuns are all black and huddled, and the bishops are going like ghosts. In the background you can see the traces of where the streets have been. All has been demolished . . . That woman looks back at something which has already disappeared . . . In one part of the picture you get the feeling of the *malaise* and the bestiality so often found among human beings today in their relationships with one another.'

The point does not need labouring. Loneliness is one of the most common and most desolating experiences. It comes to young and old alike. It is to be found in the midst of a crowd as well as in the isolation of a bed-sitter.

Jesus Christ knew that. He knew what it was to be utterly alone. He endured it on the cross, when even his relationship with his heavenly Father was cut off, and he cried out in the anguish of loneliness, 'My God, my God, why hast thou forsaken me?' (Matthew 27: 46). It was therefore all the more significant that his parting words to his disciples should have been directed towards meeting this very problem of loneliness. The risen Lord said to them, as he sent them out on their world mission, 'Be assured, I am with you always, to the end of time' (Matthew 28: 20, NEB).

The early Christians found this to be true. They became deeply conscious that Christ was with them and had, by his Spirit, come to live within their personalities. So this emphasis by the unknown writer to the Hebrews is quite characteristic of apostolic Christianity, 'Do not live for money; be content with what you have; for God himself has said, "I will never leave you or desert you"; and so we can take courage and say, "The Lord is my helper, I will not fear; what can man do to me?"' (Hebrews 13:5, 6, NEB). Jesus gave his followers the right to call him *friend* (John 15:15), and Christian experience down the centuries has shown that he does stand with them in loneliness, and that his friendship does transform the whole of life.

When I went to South Africa some time ago, a church-going student came to see me. She was a healthy extrovert, you would have thought, without a care in the world. In point of fact she was haunted by the fear of death. I explained to her about Christ's resurrection, and the difference this made to the Christian's attitude to death. Later I got a letter from her, in which she told me that she had not then been a committed Christian, as I had thought, but had since become one. Now she could write, 'Ever since that day, Christ has become more and more real to me. It's just too wonderful for words. I can't stop thinking how lucky I am to have Jesus as a friend.'

An English undergraduate wrote to me in much the same vein. 'Jesus is the only person with whom I can communicate in every situation, knowing immediately that he has understood completely. . . . I find it difficult to believe that he loves me and cares about the smallest as well as the largest details of my life; that he is willing and able to forgive me time and again for doing what I know to be wrong, and therefore what hurts him. But experience has shown that all this is true, and I am assured it always will be.'

That is what makes the Christian independent of the approbation or disapproval of the crowd. He is not squeezed into a conventional mould by the pressures of public opinion or social custom. He has a different point of reference. For he is like Charles Kingsley, who, when asked the most significant thing about his life, replied, 'I had a Friend'.

Surely a friend who can put us right with God, strengthen us in our weaknesses, find us in our lostness, give us joy, direction and companionship is a friend worth knowing. And life shared with him is life worth living.

CHAPTER SEVEN

A LIFE THAT LASTS

AT THE END of the previous chapter I mentioned a South African student, who, despite her cheery exterior, was haunted by the fear of death. I do not believe she was unusual in this respect, though she may have been more articulate about her apprehension than many others are. The truth of the matter is that death has replaced sex as the forbidden subject of conversation in polite society. In an age which has learned more than any other about the meaning of life, we still seem unable to contemplate the enigma of death. It is a subject from which we shy away. When we do mention it, we wrap it up. The mortuary is a 'chapel of rest', the cemetery a 'garden of repose'. We have not, it is true, travelled as far in this escapism as the Americans, of whom Arthur Koestler shrewdly observed that 'morticians endeavour to transform the dead, with lipstick and rouge, into horizontal members of a perennial cocktail party'. But there is no denying the fact that we run away from thinking about death; it is too disturbing. So we continue to live as though we did not have to die. We short-sightedly concentrate on enjoying the present and leave the future to look after itself.

Yet a humanism that ends at death has no answer to the most certain fact as well as the greatest problem about human life – its ending. It is not in the least fortuitous that in our day the rise of atheistic humanism should have coincided with the decline of religion and the increasing attempt to brush the ugly fact of death under the carpet. They are integrally connected. Once lose grip on the Christian faith in the risen Lord, and inevitably the spectre of death becomes more terrifying.

Some humanists make a brave show of despising death, like Bertrand Russell, who wrote, 'I am not young, and I love life. But I should scorn to shiver with terror at the thought of annihilation.' He may, of course, be the exception to Rousseau's dictum, 'He who pretends to face death without fear is a liar'. It is surely much nearer the truth, as Dr Johnson bluntly affirmed, that 'no rational man can die without uneasy apprehension'. Why is this? Epicurus, the Greek philosopher, gave this extremely revealing answer: 'What men fear is not that death is annihilation, *but that it is not!*' W. B. Yeats, in his poem *Death*, makes much the same point for our own generation:

> 'Nor dread nor hope attend
> A dying animal;
> A man awaits his end
> Dreading and hoping all.'

Another great contemporary poet, T. S. Eliot, has put his finger on what gives death its terror, in these lines in *Murder in the Cathedral*:

'. . . behind the face of Death the Judgment
And behind the Judgment, the Void, more horrid than
   active shapes of hell;
Emptiness, absence, separation from God;
The horror of the effortless journey to the empty land
Which is no land, only emptiness, absence, the Void,
Where those who were men can no longer turn the mind
To distraction, delusion, escape into dreams, pretence. . .'

How does the resurrection of Jesus Christ affect this universal dread? It makes all the difference.

Jesus assured his followers that their destiny is linked irrevocably with his own. He said, 'In my Father's house are many rooms; if it were not so, would I have told you that I go to prepare a place for you? And when I go and prepare a place for you, I will come again and will take you to myself, that where I am you may be also' (John 14:2, 3). His resurrection showed that what he had promised, he was able to perform.

Does this Christian talk about a future life sound like wish fulfilment? I do not think so. There is nothing so very wonderful about being assured of an endless existence: it could be very boring. Taken by itself, the idea of endless life could be more terrible than joyful. As Lord Boothby observed in *What I Believe*, 'Nor do I wish it [*i.e.*, immortality]. The thought of a spiritual Boothby twanging a spiritual harp for eternity has, for me, limited attractions.' Of course it has! It was John Baillie who pointed out, shrewdly, when commenting on pagan views of immortality, 'Nobody ever wanted an endless *quantity* of life until discovery had been made of a new and quite particular and exceptional *quality* of life.' He refers, of course, to the risen life of Christ, which the Christian begins to share now, and continues to enjoy hereafter. It is this that gives us the thrill of confident expectation as we think about death. Dr Baillie gives a delightful story in his book, *And the Life Everlasting*, from which I have just quoted, which powerfully makes this point that the essence of the Christian hope of immortality is continued relationship with Jesus himself.

An old man lay dying, and he asked his Christian doctor 'if he had any convictions as to what awaited him in the life beyond. The doctor fumbled for an answer. But ere he could speak, there was heard a scratching at the door and his answer was given him. "Do you hear that?" he asked his patient. "That is my dog. I left him downstairs, but he grew impatient and has come up here and hears my voice. He has no notion of what is inside this door, but he knows that I am here. Now is it not the same with you? You do not know what lies beyond the Door, but you know that your Master is there."'

I heard recently a similar story from Dr Cicely Saunders, a world authority on the care of the dying. She was lecturing on the subject, and spoke about many of her patients. But one in particular sticks in my mind. She was called Louie.

She had had a grim life. Born with such brittle bones that if she moved suddenly they would break, she had spent all her life in bed. At length she died of cancer. If anyone had good cause to complain about her lot, you might have thought it would have been she. But so far from making her lose her faith in God, her sufferings seem only to have deepened it. Dr Saunders had several conversations with her about their common Christian faith, and its relevance to the plight that Louie was in.

One day she asked Louie, when talking about meeting the Lord at death, 'And when it really happens, what's the first thing that you'll say to him?' Louie's reply was instantaneous, 'Oh, I'll say, "*I know you.*"'

That is the heart of the Christian faith about the future. The One we know by faith now, we shall know face to face then. This confidence is grounded solidly on the fact that Jesus rose. That is what enables Christians to face death not merely with stoical resignation, but with joyful anticipation: 'Happy are the dead who die in the faith of Christ!' (Revelation 14: 13, NEB).

What that life will be like we cannot say in any detail, nor need we try. Perhaps the nearest we can get to it is contained in two hints in 1 Corinthians 15. Paul has been talking about the resurrection of Jesus, and makes this the ground for what he has to say about the resurrection of Christians. There are, as he sees it, two representative men in the history of the world, two men whose actions were decisive for the whole human race: Adam, whose physical nature we do share, and Christ, whose risen nature we shall share. 'Just as we have borne the image of the man of dust, we shall also bear the image of the man of heaven' (1 Corinthians 15: 49). We shall be like the risen Lord. That is our destiny.

Notice carefully what Paul has to say at this point. He is not arguing for the Christian's merely spiritual survival. That would not have needed emphasizing at Corinth or any other Greek city. Immortality of the soul was taken for granted. But it is resurrection of the body that Paul is telling them about. Not, of course, a crass resuscitation, as though by some magic men rise from their tombs (warts and all) to their resurrection life. Far from it. But resurrection will be bodily resurrection, just as Jesus' was. It will involve the whole personality. There are, as Paul points out, various different kinds of bodies, equipping their owners for life in different environments – one sort of body enabling fish to live in water, another for animals on dry land, and yet another for birds in the air. Similarly, God proposes to give us a body enabling us to live a spiritual existence. It will have continuity with our present body, but will not be subject to the limitations of time and space any more than the body of the risen Jesus was. 'If there is a physical body, there is also a spiritual body' (1 Corinthians 15:44). The risen body of Jesus is both the proof of this assertion, and the only model we have for imagining what that body, that vehicle for expressing our personality, will be like.

The relation between what we are now and what we shall be then is well expressed in another passage in this chapter: and this is our second hint of what the life hereafter will be like. Paul says, 'But some one will ask, "How are the dead raised? With what kind of body do they come?" You foolish man! What you sow does not come to life unless it dies. And what you sow is not the body which is to be, but a bare kernel, perhaps of wheat or of some other grain. But God gives it a body as he has chosen, and to each kind of seed its own body' (1 Corinthians 15:35–38). What a marvellous illustration!

If you had never seen a pea-plant in your life, imagine the surprise you would have when, having put that small, dry, shrivelled seed into the ground, in three months' time you came back to find a fine healthy green plant, complete with pods full of peas! If you had not yet got *blasé* about this annual miracle, you would be deeply impressed at the transformation of the life of that pea. The full-grown plant contains the same life that you put into the ground as a seed which would die; but that life has far greater possibilities now, and far greater splendour.

That is what it is going to be like in the resurrection. We shall have a continuity of life with what we are now; we shall have a recognizable likeness. But our whole being will be transformed; new vistas of opportunity will open up to us in this new dimension of existence. Such, at least, is God's promise. That is, if you like, what is written on the outside of the packet. And how are we to know if what is written on the packet is true? How are we to be sure about this remarkable and, one might think, entirely improbable future that it predicts for the peas? The answer is simple. One single pea would be enough to settle the matter. If one pea out of that packet were actually planted, and rose out of its death in the earth to give substance to the promises on the packet, then we should have every reason to believe that the rest of the seeds would grow. That is precisely the assurance which the resurrection of Jesus gives us. This one member of our humanity who has died and risen gives substance to the promises of God about our destiny. He rose: we shall rise. And when we do, we shall be like him (1 John 3: 2). Not a mere spiritual survival, not a crude materialist resuscitation, but a complete transformation, such as the body of Jesus underwent at his resurrection. That is what the Christian has to look forward to. This was the transformation Dietrich Bonhoeffer was thinking about in the closing months of his life. He was a distinguished German theologian, imprisoned by Hitler in the World War II, and executed on 8 April, 1945. Before being taken out to his death, he conducted a service for his fellow prisoners at their request, and this was his text. 'Praise be to the God and Father of our Lord Jesus Christ, who in his mercy gave us new birth into a living hope by the resurrection of Jesus Christ from the dead!' (1 Peter 1: 3, NEB). And as the guards removed him, he sent this last message to the Bishop of Chichester, 'This is the end – but for me the beginning of life.'

That is the authentic Christian attitude in the face of death. It is shared by one who fought on the other side to Germany in the same World War. Wing-Commander Branse Burbridge won two DSOs and two DFCs for his night-fighter exploits over Germany. Rawnsley and Wright, the authors of the bestselling paperback *Night Fighter*, make his story the climax of their book. The team of Burbridge and Skelton (another Christian, now a vicar in the East End) became the most skilful in the business, and established a record bag of enemy aircraft for any one crew of night-fighters. Here are men who flirted with death time and again. Their attitude to it is most revealing. This is how Branse described the experience of his first dog-fight:

'In our first real scrap, our opponent seemed to be out-turning me; I turned tighter than ever and banked very steeply – this "toppled" the instruments, which would take twenty minutes to reset themselves. So even if he didn't get us first, we might spin into the sea. . . . I felt prickly – I was afraid. Then something hit me, but it wasn't a bullet! In a split second, it must have been, I realized two things: both stemmed from the fact that I was a Christian.

'First, if God had further work for me to do for him after the war, I was bound to survive; second, if I did get killed, death would be literally the gateway to heaven, and I should see the Lord Jesus Christ. So what did it matter?'

He continued, reflectively, 'The new life that Jesus Christ has given me is *eternal*, and so I need not be afraid of death. In fact, I have not been afraid since then. But it took that dog-fight at night over Germany to make me see this.

'When I leave this earth I shall live eternal life in Christ's presence. Whilst I am here I live it "at a distance". Through it, he has taught me so many lessons, guided me through so many problems, given me so much satisfaction, spoken to me so often, that my belief in the living Christ could never be destroyed. Try telling a pilot at an overseas station that the RAF does not exist – and he'll tell you you are talking through your helmet!'

Here is a man who was able to face death unafraid, because of his relationship with the risen Christ. That same relationship, meanwhile, gives zest and direction to his living. He helped to bring the Inter-School Christian Fellowship into existence after the war and took on its leadership. Now, nearly twenty years later, the ISCF operates in over two thousand secondary schools of all types, and has been the agency through which thousands of boys and girls have been brought to know the living Christ.

Branse Burbridge's story is just one among many that show the practical relevance of the resurrection to a man's attitude to death and consequently to his approach to life. The two are aptly brought together by St Paul in the closing verses of his great chapter on the resurrection, 1 Corinthians 15. They stress the Christian's proper enjoyment of this world and sense of purpose in it as he works for Christ, coupled with his joyful anticipation of a fuller life with Christ after death. 'And when our mortality has been clothed with immortality, then the saying of Scripture will come true: "Death is swallowed up; victory is won!" "O Death, where is your victory? O Death, where is your sting?"' (1 Corinthians 15: 54, 55, NEB).

That is the Christian confidence for the future. And for the present, 'Therefore, my beloved brothers, stand firm and immovable, and work for the Lord always, work without limit, since you know that in the Lord your labour cannot be lost' (1 Corinthians 15: 58, NEB).

CHAPTER EIGHT

MEN ALIVE!

FROM THE COMMITTED . . .

THE EARLY CHRISTIANS were not judges: they were advocates. They did not try to assess the value of Christianity, or compare it with paganism; they were passionate in their devotion to Jesus and in their recommendation of him to others. This was the inevitable outcome of their own experience. 'For if a man is in Christ he becomes a new person altogether – the past is finished and gone, everything has become fresh and new' (2 Corinthians 5: 17, Phillips).

In comparison with this new life which they experienced, their old existence seemed a mere shadow. This is how they expressed it: 'God has given men eternal life and this real life is to be found only in his Son. It follows naturally that any man who has genuine contact with Christ has this life; and if he has not, then he does not possess this life at all' (1 John 5: 11, 12, Phillips).

These early believers found in Christ a new vitality which they had not known before; they became filled with the same sort of love that Jesus had for others; and they gradually found their very habits being transformed by their companionship with him.

It is the same today. Despite much formalism and nominal Christianity in the churches, all over the world you will find these same characteristics of men who have become new people, of men who have found life; they possess a vitality, a quality of character, and a love they never had before. And they are enthusiastic advocates for the Christ through whom this change comes about.

A changed character

Here is an example of the change that Jesus makes to a man's character once he is allowed access. Fred was a Cockney; conceited, illiterate and tough. He was, as he himself put it, 'an embryo gangster, already with a list of crimes which society could level against me, and sins which accused me of their own accord'. The story of Fred's conversion is fascinating in itself, but the sequel is even more interesting. He is now an Army padre. This is what he has to say about the revolution which has taken place in his life.

'The living Christ has given me what no court, no psychiatrist, no probation officer, and certainly not my own conscience could give me – the consciousness of sins forgiven. The living Christ has given me a sense that he understands and cares for me, which no other friendship has ever fulfilled. This alone has been of enormous therapeutic value to my scarred soul.

'The proof of the pudding is in the eating. The proof of the existence of a living Christ is in a personal relationship with him. My experience of him since my conversion has been varied, and with trials enough to make me very sure of him. Army life, on active service with the Parachute Brigade in various parts of the world, has removed the possibility of my faith being due to weak sentimentality. The harsh reality of fighting the continually exposed weaknesses in my own character (in particular, refusal to acknowledge my limitations, coupled with smugness and self-assertion) has dismissed the possibility of my experience being merely emotional. Emotion does not sustain the continuing effort needed to suppress the passions which war against the soul.

'The personal discipline that education and character training have demanded of me is not likely to have sprung from wishful thinking! The joy of a loving wife, two children, and a secure and happy home, have shown me that through the living Christ even one who, like myself, was once described by a magistrate as a "social menace" can be made more than just tolerable. That is something of the difference that Jesus Christ has made, and continues to make, to me.'

That is the testimony of one of the most complete men's men it has ever been my privilege to meet: paratrooper, army soccer player, boxing champion, and so on. All Fred's potential gangsterlike propensities have been taken over, redirected, and used by Jesus Christ. This is what Jesus Christ can do in making new men of us. What other force is there in the world that can do the same?

A new vitality

Fred's story reminds us of the transformations in character which we meet in the New Testament Epistles. And the same sheer joy in living that we find there is a notable feature in many Christians today. This is how one friend of mine expressed it.

'When I became a Christian, five years ago, my mates on the building site misunderstood what had happened to me. They thought I'd "got religion". They were sure it would soon wear off. But they couldn't have been more wrong. I didn't suddenly become religious or very keen on church. But I did find that the risen Jesus was beginning to make a real difference to my life. When I came to know Jesus, I started to enjoy work, and even mixing mortar and building walls became exciting.'

There is something very telling about that last sentence. The ordinary things of life took on a new look when undertaken with Jesus as Companion. The same point stands out in the case of a Lloyd's underwriter who was an expert yachtsman and simply lived for boats. Since becoming a Christian he has found a complete change of priorities in his life. No longer does the boat come first. Christ is the dominating power and the driving force in his life. 'Before, it was a matter of looking forward to the week-end or the next race. But now it is a thrill just to be alive, and even little things like washing up and house-work are fun!'

Perhaps the most impressive example of this increased joy in living, even in the midst of appalling circumstances, is to be found in a story published not long ago in *The Christian*. Eighteen prisoners in Pulau Senang prison, off Singapore, had incited a riot among the other prisoners. The revolt was quelled in due course, and they were tried, convicted, and sentenced to death.

A Methodist minister, the Rev. Khoo Siaw Wah, spent a lot of time among these men, bringing to them the Christian gospel. So effectively did he do so, that before their death fifteen of the eighteen had professed faith in Christ. Before their execution, all of them signed this letter to the minister:

'Our dear Rev. Khoo,

We do thank you from the bottom of our hearts . . . for all you have done for us. You were everything in our hour of need. You were the beacon that guided us to the haven of Jesus Christ. You taught us to have unquestion-ing faith in God's Word . . ., to pray to him, to ask for his forgiveness . . . During these long agonizing months of mental torture . . . till now we stand at the very brink of death, at the very edge of eternity, you have given us so much of yourself in selfless devotion. It is through you that we now look death in the face with courage and calm-ness, for we doubt not God's promise of forgiveness by the simple act of belief and acceptance. We know that in three and one half hour's time when we pass from off this earth, our Lord and Saviour Jesus Christ will be waiting with open arms to lead us to our new home in the house of the Father . . . With our dying breath we once again affirm to you our undying gratitude – gratitude that will transcend even death itself.

Fare you well, our dear Rev.,
Yours in Christ,
[Eighteen signatures]'

Here were men that were *fully alive* as they came up to death. They provide an up-to-date commentary on Jesus' words, 'I am the resurrection and the life; he who believes in me, though he die, yet shall he live, and whoever lives and believes in me shall never die' (John 11: 25, 26).

A deep love

One of the things that made an enormous impression on the ancient world was the deep love and concern that these Christians had, not only for each other, but for those outside their number. 'Look how these Christians love one another' was originally not said in mockery but in tribute. Such love for others is the logical consequence of sharing the life of the risen Jesus. He was love incarnate, and if Christians did not share something of his concern for the needy and the unevangelized, there would be something very wrong. Here are two modern examples of the way in which Christ's love grips people and goes out from them.

One evening in 1951 Allyn Cooke, a missionary who for love of Christ had gone to work in North Thailand, asked a village headman, Brother Six, for a night's shelter. The man had never heard of God, and was a slave to opium addiction. Before he went to rest, the missionary spoke briefly to him about the great God who made man, Jesus Christ who died for man, and the Holy Spirit who can change man and break the power of evil habits.

Some time afterwards Brother Six put his faith in the Christ of whom he had heard. On his next visit to the village, Cooke found him rejoicing in the faith, and already breaking with opium. Brother Six looked at the animistic life-bands on his wrists. 'I'm a Christian now. What need have I of these?' he asked. He threw the life-bands away, and then tore down and burnt the demon-shelf in the house, whilst his heathen neighbours watched in terror. After giving him a great deal of opposition, his wife, too, became a Christian.

On Easter Sunday, 1964, Brother Six was ordained. Seventy Yao believers, most of whom had been converted through his agency, came to witness the ordination. Brother Six is now a grandfather, and feels his responsibility of shepherding his family and the five hundred Yao believers in the fourteen villages round about. But he has a wider vision of service than that. He tape-records messages about the Lord for fellow tribesmen who are refugees in Vietnam and Laos. 'They say it was the Communists who drove them out of the north', he explains. 'But I believe it was God who led them to a place where they can hear the gospel and be saved. Pray that God will open the way for some of us to go and witness to them.' Such is the love which Christ implants in a man who becomes a Christian.

The second instance I want to mention comes from the other side of the world. In January 1956 five missionaries, who had been seeking to bring the Christian gospel to the Auca Indians (a savage, stone-age tribe in the heart of Ecuador) were speared to death. Ten years later, in 1966, some of the Auca converts to Christianity, including Kimo, one of the killers, visited Britain to tell of the change that the risen Lord had brought into their lives. They had been won over by the love and dedication of the closest relations of the martyred missionaries. Women like Elizabeth Elliot and Rachel Saint refused to let their bereavement make them bitter. They determined to press on in the attempt to reach these ignorant tribesmen with the good news. They went to live and labour among them, and in due time the selfless love which radiated out from these dedicated women won the majority of this small tribe to Christ. Interestingly enough, the first to come to faith among the Aucas were the men who actually did the killings. One of them, Gikita, said simply, 'I used to hate and kill, but now the Lord has healed my heart'. Such is their love for others, such their concern to pass on to others the gospel that has made new men of them, that they are now risking their lives to tell of the Saviour to a neighbouring tribe of Indians with whom they have had a blood feud from time immemorial.

All the world over, those who have taken the step of penitent surrender to Jesus Christ recommend him with confidence to others. They become what the New Testament calls 'ambassadors for Christ'. They assert from their own experience, as well as from the Scriptures, that a new dimension of life awaits any man who is prepared to follow Christ. It is indeed the case that 'if a man is in Christ he becomes a new person altogether – the past is finished and gone, everything has become fresh and new' (2 Corinthians 5: 17, Phillips).

. . . TO THE UNCOMMITTED

We live in a day when such enthusiastic advocacy of *any* cause, let alone a religious one, is unfashionable. The majority of people prefer to be spectators rather than participants. This is true of politics; it is true, too, of social service. Many youth clubs are desperate for lack of leaders; many 'Meals on Wheels' clubs for the aged are crying out for helpers. I have noticed in visiting a large mental hospital fairly regularly how comparatively few patients get visited by their friends and relations. It seems that people are anxious not to involve themselves in something rather embarrassing, a side of life they would rather forget. Even in sport we have got into the parlous condition, as a nation, of preferring to watch it than to take part in it. Enthusiasm is out: 'spectatoritis' is in.

This unwillingness to be actively involved is one of the marks of the contemporary deadness which we examined in Chapter One. We saw there that it was much the same in Athens in the first century, where Paul's preaching of Jesus and the resurrection caused such a stir. It intrigued them so much that they gave Paul a chance to present his case at a formal occasion on the ancient hill of Areopagus, just outside the city. He certainly had an interesting audience. It comprised not only the happy-go-lucky gossips, always out for some piece of news, but the philosophers of the day as well. The Stoics were the 'duty-first-and-keep-a-stiff-upper-lip' types. The Epicureans were the 'happiness-is-all-that-matters' crowd. They were intelligent and *avant-garde*. How was he to approach this formidable audience?

He gave them a very surprising, very unfashionable and very peremptory command. They must repent. God, he said, had 'winked at' the times of ignorance of himself in which the Athenians had lived so long. But now there was no excuse for continued ignorance. God had taken human nature upon him, in the man Jesus. And this man, the proper man, challenged them to ally themselves to him if they were truly come of age, as they fondly imagined they were. God, Paul told them, 'now . . . commands all men everywhere to repent' (Acts 17:30).

God might very well have left it there. After all, if it is *God* who tells men they must repent, only a fool would ignore it. But God did not leave it there. He gave a reason for the command. It is 'because he has fixed the day on which he will have the world judged, and justly judged, by a man of his choosing' (Acts 17:31, NEB). God will judge us all one day; it will be absolutely fair. We will be judged by no alien standard, but by what it means to be fully alive, fully human. The standard will be man as he ought to be, Jesus. His love will show up our hate, his unselfishness our greed, his purity our lust, his courage our cowardice, his integrity our deceit. We shall be compared with him. That is why it is so important to repent and get rightly related to him. Otherwise we shall inevitably be rejected by the upright Judge of all the earth.

'Ah,' we can almost hear the Athenians say, 'but how can we believe in any judgment? It all seems highly improbable to us!' Paul had his answer ready. He continued, 'Of this he has given assurance to all men by raising him from the dead.' The argument runs like this. The judgment is as certain as the resurrection. Paul argues from a past certainty to a future one. The incarnate Jesus attested his claims to deity by the (as yet future) event of the resurrection. The apostle Paul attested the reality of future judgment by the (now past) event of the resurrection. The resurrection is certain; the judgment is certain. And because no man can evade it, God commands all men everywhere to repent and entrust themselves to the one who died for them and rose again.

The story is told of an exhibition of Rembrandt's paintings. It was closing time, and as the custodian moved people out of the gallery, he heard some of the crowd making derogatory remarks about the artist and his work. He remarked quietly, 'It is not the artist, but the viewers who are on trial.' The same is true of Jesus Christ. You are free to mock him, if you wish, as some of the Athenians did. By all means mock at a God who can raise the dead — if you dare. You are entitled to put off a decision, if you wish, as some of the Athenians did on that occasion. But remember that the God who offers himself to you in love will one day confront you in judgment. He is not to be trifled with. Moreover, it is you, not he, who is on trial. Christ's integrity and person have been vindicated by the resurrection. He faces you as the Ideal Man, who can impart newness of life to you. The question is, what will you do with him?

Damaris and Dionysius and some others at Athens committed themselves fully to Jesus, and joined up with his church. Men have done so down the centuries, and have not been disappointed. If you take this step of putting your life in his hands, you will discover in your own experience the reality of the resurrection. This is how two African students put it. One writes, 'I know Jesus lives because four years ago I claimed his promise, "Him that cometh to me I will in no wise cast out". And that promise has proved true in my experience. I have increasingly realized his presence with me.' The other man writes of the 'sin and havoc, the shame and unrest' in his life as he toyed with the Christian message without repenting and responding to Christ. Then one night he gave in to God. He asked the Lord to accept him. 'He responded, and I had peace. Since then I have seen Christ answer prayer in many ways. I have seen his hand in some major decisions I have had to make. To me he is real, and I know him. He speaks to me. But I cannot prove it to anyone else. It is a thing to be experienced. I think anyone who really wants to know if Jesus is alive must begin where I did by sincerely and wholeheartedly accepting the claims of Christ and see what happens. It works.'

Yes, it works. And it all begins when a man or woman ventures out on that lonely meeting with the risen Christ. This is an encounter that cannot be bypassed. After all, the only way to verify *anyone's* existence is to meet him. Of course, there are records that vouch for a person's existence. He has acquaintances who will tell you that he is alive. But you cannot strike up any sort of relationship with such a man unless you meet him. There is no other way.

It is very much like that with Jesus Christ. The records vouch for his continued existence; so do a great many present-day witnesses. But the only way for you to be sure about it is to meet him for yourself.

Admittedly, you cannot see him. But is this so great a difficulty? You cannot see the wind either, and yet you can experience it and be very much aware of its results. That is an illustration Jesus himself gave of Christian commitment, the encounter which makes so radical a difference to a man that he called it nothing less than a new birth (John 3 : 7, 8). After all, it was no easier for most of the early Christians (who were not eyewitnesses) to commit themselves to Jesus than it is for us. Yet they did it. Peter could write to believers all over Asia Minor, Pontus, Cappadocia, Bithynia and so on, confident that they all had this identical experience of knowing one they could not see – not just knowing about him, but *knowing* him. He wrote, 'You have not seen him, yet you love him; and trusting in him now without seeing him, you are transported with a joy too great for words, while you reap the harvest of your faith, that is, salvation for your souls' (1 Peter 1 : 8, 9, NEB).

Interestingly enough, we have a sidelight on these very people from a dispassionate source – none other than the

Roman Governor of Bithynia, Pliny the Younger. He wrote in AD 112 to the Emperor, asking his advice on how far to carry the persecution of the Christians. Incidentally, his letter gives us fascinating glimpses of their growth, their fellowship, their faith, their joy. They used to meet early in the morning on a fixed day, to sing a hymn to Christ as God; they bound themselves to live blameless lives; they remained steadfast in their Christian allegiance even in the face of execution; and their numbers increased so much in towns and villages throughout the province that the pagan festivals had been discontinued, and the pagan temples deserted (Pliny, *Letters* x. 96).

Have you got a first-hand faith like that? Has the risen Jesus turned you into one of these men who have come fully alive? If not, the remedy lies with you. Jesus has promised, 'The man who comes to me I will never turn away' (John 6: 37, NEB). When you take that promise seriously, and put your life in his hands, you will know for certain that the resurrection is true. Until then, you will remain in the ranks of the unconvinced, and the uncommitted.

A SUGGESTED PRAYER OF COMMITMENT

Lord Jesus Christ, I believe you became man so as to reveal God to me. I believe you died on the cross for my sins. I believe you rose from the tomb and are alive today. I am ashamed of having kept you at a distance for so long, and I acknowledge that I do not in the least deserve your love. Yet I thankfully accept your offer to come and share life with me, and to bring me into God's family. I am prepared for what it will cost me to be a Christian, at home, at work, and in the conflict with my own weaknesses. I am prepared for it, because I trust your promise that you will stand by me and strengthen me. So here I am, Lord, at your disposal. You promised, 'The man who comes to me I will never turn away'. I claim my part in that promise, and I thank you from the bottom of my heart for accepting me. Now please use me in your church for your glory. Amen.